# A Disciplined Life

EMMANUEL ADEWUSI

Cover Design: Timothy Paul Designs
ISBN-13: 9780995349261
ISBN-10: 0995349266

# DEDICATION

*To the team God has assembled for this project, thank you for your tireless efforts in ensuring this work is excellent. Thank you Victor Owunne, Tumininu Ojelade and Mariam Pondamali.*

*To Rev. George Adegboye, thank you sir for accepting to write the foreword to this book at a moment's notice. Thank you for the divine seal of approval.*

*To my wife, Pastor Ibukun Adewusi, thank you for keeping me accountable. Thank you for joining me on this journey to be more disciplined.*

*To my counselor, friend, teacher and coach, the Holy Spirit, I am blessed to have you on my side. Thank you for letting me in on the secret that led to this book.*

# TABLE OF CONTENT

# FOREWORD

By far, the most common roadblock that Satan puts in our way is the problem of discipline. This lack of discipline can have disastrous effects on our destiny, if not well managed. The Bible says in Proverbs 5:23 (NIV), *"For lack of discipline they will die, led astray by their own great folly."* Self-control and self-discipline are also key factors in any success you hope to have in this life. Without self-discipline, you are unlikely to achieve anything of lasting value. The apostle Paul realized this when he wrote, *"Every athlete in training submits to strict discipline, in order to be crowned with a wreath that will not last; but we do it for one that will last forever"* (1 Corinthians 9:25 GNT).

Olympic athletes train for years in order to have a chance to win a brief moment of glory. But the race we are running is far more important than any earthly athletic event. Therefore, self-control is not optional for Christians, as is evident in 1 Corinthians 9:25. Daniel had to make a choice, to either eat the king's food or control his appetite. Daniel chose the latter. Many teenagers of today wouldn't have made that choice. Think about it. At age 15, you are forcefully taken from your home country and you may never see your parents again. Then you find yourself in a foreign country with no parental supervision, and the most powerful man in that country offers you all kinds of perks and says, "I'm going to give you power, prestige, and pleasure. You'll get the best of everything."

Could this be turned down? Many children have been ruined by too early and too much success, but this was not the case for Daniel. He was incredibly disciplined for a 15-year-old child, who was isolated from his parents.

Daniel reflected what Paul wrote hundreds of years later, when he said in Romans 6:13 (NLT): "*Do not let any part of your body become a tool of wickedness, to be used for sinning. Instead, give yourself completely to God . . . as a tool to do what is right for the glory of God.*" For Daniel, a lack of discipline would mean forfeiting God's unique plan for his life. Daniel wouldn't do that. So, he tells the representative of the most powerful man in the world, Nebuchadnezzar, that he was not going to conform to him because he was Jewish and not Babylonian. That is maturity and discipline, particularly for a 15-year-old. When we are disciplined, obedient, and following God's will, we will be successful in God's eyes.

As believers we are all in a race. The Bible says in 1 Corinthians 9:24-26 (TLB), "*In a race everyone runs, but only one person gets first prize. So run your race to win. To win the contest you must deny yourselves many things that would keep you from doing your best. An athlete goes to all this trouble just to win a blue ribbon or a silver cup, but we do it for a heavenly reward that never disappears. So I run straight to the goal with purpose in every step. I fight to win.*"

As those in a race, we should strive not to get sidelined or run off into a ditch. It is important we make it to the finish line and win the prize. As athletes, a few things are important to us, if it's our desire to be our best. Top on the list must be that we intend to win. This is the difference between being a casual Christian and a committed Christian.

The difference lies in the
going to win in life, it's gc
to happen by accident or ·
about being who God m
discipline ourselves. N
out training. You don't.
feel like doing. There are no su.
no shortcuts to greatness. There are go..
we need do without, so we can spend more tir..
It's only then that we must stay focused on the rewaru.
can handle enormous pain and discipline in life, if we realize
there's a purpose for it and that there's going to be a payoff
at the end. The Bible says in Hebrews 12:2 (MSG), *"Keep your
eyes on Jesus, who both began and finished this race we're in. Study how
he did it. Because he never lost sight of where he was headed — that
exhilarating finish in and with God — he could put up with anything
along the way: Cross, shame, whatever. And now he's there, in the place
of honor, right alongside God."*

In his book, "The Effective Executive", Peter Drucker
says that, "every time one meets a person with great strengths,
one is also meeting someone with great weaknesses." In our
world today, we all know about the celebrities, athletes, and
even presidents who, although they had tremendous strengths,
also had a weakness in their character that ultimately led to
their downfall. In spite of the fact that they were very strong,
they let a weakness destroy their lives. It is a pity, but also true
that self-indulgence in the form of lack of self-control or undisciplined living, will weaken us. It can be the way we spend
money, indulge in sex, eat food, consume alcohol, express

r manage time. Indeed, anything that's left out

weaken our lives.

seem like just a small thing, but the fact is, small
n have an enormous impact on our lives. We can-
ulge little weaknesses and assume they won't eventually
over and weaken us entirely. It doesn't make any differ-
ce what area of our life is out of control. It's just a question
of time before that lack of control begins to undermine the
way we live for God. *"Do not be misled. Remember that you cannot
ignore God and get away with it. A man will always reap just the kind
of crop he sows. If he sows to please his own desires, he will be planting
seeds of evil and will surely reap a harvest of spiritual decay and death"*
(Galatians 6: 7-8 TLB).

In the end, where can we find the strength to build discipline back into our life? It is by deliberately giving our weaknesses to Jesus, and then, taking the steps he tells us to take
(i.e. as he tells us to take them, how he tells us to take them,
and when he tells us to take them). *"And that about wraps it up.
God is strong, and he wants you strong"* (Ephesians 6:10 MSG).
That is the kernel of this book.

**Reverend George O. Adegboye**
**President, Ever Increasing Word Ministries**
**(Rhema Chapel International Churches Worldwide)**

# PREFACE

This book was born when the Lord said to me, "you are not disciplined enough for the level that I am taking you to." This set me on a course to examine what discipline really is, and how I can be more disciplined for the next level.

In this book, we will review the different aspects of our lives that we must cultivate discipline in order to excel, and be all that God created us to be and do.

I pray that the words in this book will come alive in your heart.

Since grace can be imparted through words, I pray that the words from this book will impart the grace to live a disciplined life upon you.

It is not as hard as you think.

Enjoy the ride.

**Emmanuel Adewusi**

# INTRODUCTION

Have you ever pictured how far you can go? Have you ever imagined the limits of your achievement in this life? Have you ever imagined how productive you can be in all areas of your life (e.g. spiritual, financial, social)? Have you ever wished you had more time in the day?

In many cases, the missing link to extraordinary attainment is discipline. Human beings were not created to live a restraint-free life. If that were to be the case, there would be no laws to follow. Laws such as: the law of gravity, sowing and reaping, law of lift, etc., would be non-existent if humans were not expected to live under well-defined principles.

Throughout history, the scientific study of the universe has plainly shown the disciplined nature of planets. This is evident through the way in which the earth rotates around the sun, the moon rotates around the earth, the way seasons follow one another, etc. All of these elements are conducted in a disciplined and consistent manner.

Our society on the other hand, seems out of control. Many lack the vital inner discipline needed to succeed. 2 Timothy 3:1-5 goes on to say, *"But mark this: There will be terrible times in the last days. People will be lovers of themselves, lovers of money, boastful, proud, abusive, disobedient to their parents, ungrateful, unholy, without love, unforgiving, slanderous, without self-control, brutal, not lovers of the good, treacherous, rash, conceited, lovers of pleasure rather than lovers of God, having a form of godliness but denying its power."* If you skimmed over the list, thinking you knew them all, you might have missed "without self-control." Most of the evil behaviors in the list above stems from the absence of self-control.

Christians should stand out as different from the evil ones who are fulfilling biblical prophecy. Jesus said, *"By this all men will know that you are my disciples, if you love one another"* (John 13:35).

Love, of course, is first in the list of the nine fruit of the Spirit (Galatians 5:22-23), whereas self-control is last. Self-control regulates all the preceding fruit or virtues of the Spirit.

Love without restraint becomes passion. Joy taken to excess is shallow frivolity. Peace without self-control becomes idleness. Patience without balance becomes apathy. Likewise, gentleness without balance becomes weakness; goodness without balance becomes self-serving. Faith completely without reason becomes blind superstition. Meekness taken to an extreme becomes timidity. The world speaks of love, joy, and peace, but its darkened mind knows only a false shadow of the divine reality. Christians should demonstrate self-control in this out-of-control world.

The approach I will be taking in this book is to discuss the different aspects of a person, i.e. Spirit, Soul and Body, and how discipline ought to be applied to these aspects. I will also touch on some habits that a successful person ought to imbibe.

The approach to tackle this subject from these perspectives is very important. For example, some Christians find themselves beating the air when it comes to health challenges that they face, others are quick to blame the devil, or a spiritual attack, for every adverse health condition. The same applies to emotional imbalance, and any kind of unideal situation a person might face. The best approach is to carefully assess different areas to find the root of the problem.

I once found myself feeling feverish and having chills throughout my body; it sometimes felt like the cold air was going all the way to my bones. It so happened that I was involved in a 21-days fast during that period. I could have easily interpreted that to be a spiritual attack, but instead, I took time to ask the Holy Spirit what was going on. I felt that if anyone would know the precise issue, it would be the Holy Spirit. I was right, because He told me my body was simply responding to a lack of certain vital vitamins and minerals as a result of the fast. His recommendation was to resume my intake of multivitamins, which I did, and the shivering ceased immediately.

Similarly, a person could be experiencing the same shivering and feverish conditions and conclude that it is as a result of the body lacking certain vitamins and minerals. They might find, however, that the situation continues to worsen even after the consistent intake of multivitamins. Perhaps in this case, it was a spiritual attack that multivitamins can definitely not resolve.

**Emmanuel Adewusi**

# 1

## SELF-DISCIPLINE VS. SELF-CONTROL

**Is There Any Difference?**

On the surface, it seems as though the terms *self-discipline* and *self-control* are one and the same. The distinction becomes more apparent when we remove the word "self" from both terms, which significantly changes their meaning. It is at this point that one realizes that discipline is different from control.

I define discipline as the act of bringing something under the influence of well-defined principles, while control is about domination or subordination.

Merriam-Webster defines self-discipline as the correction or regulation of oneself for the sake of improvement.

Merriam-Webster also defines self-control as the restraint exercised over one's own impulses, emotions, or desires.

Self-discipline is closely tied with having well-defined principles, while self-control is simply when subjugating something or someone without any clear connection to principles.

Self-control, plus principles (such as consistency, regularity, and routine), equals discipline. Without self-control, we cannot be disciplined. Hence, self-control is not the end, discipline is the end.

Everyone has the ability to control themselves, but not everyone is disciplined, i.e. not everyone is able to consistently and regularly control themselves. Until you do this, you are not disciplined.

Self-control alone does not bring lasting results, it is discipline that does.

Discipline is getting a new habit on an intentional cycle.

For discipline to last for a lifetime, and be an enjoyable journey, it has to be motivated by a clear vision. Any activity of discipline that is not tied to a clear motivating vision is unsustainable.

> *"Where there is no revelation, the people cast off restraint;*
> *But happy is he who keeps the law." (Proverbs 29:18)*

The word "revelation" in this passage means vision. It means that vision helps people to put the necessary restraints in place, in order to achieve the vision.

The word "law" in this passage means a strict routine; a person that keeps the routine in order to achieve the vision is a happy person. This is probably because they will continually enjoy success.

In Luke 12:49-50, Jesus said, *"I came to send fire on the earth, and how I wish it were already kindled! But I have a baptism to be baptized with, and how distressed I am till it is accomplished!"* In this passage, Jesus was emphasizing the need for discipline. He put Himself under strict conditions, so that He could accomplish His mission.

## The Concept of Drifting

This is a fundamental question that we all need to answer and understand, in order to achieve success in life.

To answer this question appropriately, we need to examine a concept called "drifting."

Hebrews 2:1 states, *"Therefore we must give the more earnest heed to the things we have heard, lest we drift away."*

Drifting is a term that refers to a state of moving away from the defined target. Many goals that do not get achieved are missed many times not because of lack of technical skill, but because the visionary got distracted.

Drifting is being in a state of distraction. This distraction is dangerous, because it robs a person of the attainment of their goals and desires. A drifter is someone who allows the good or the bad to take their attention away from the best.

An example of drifting is, you intend conveying a message to a person and you set out to do so, but you end up forgetting your original intent while conversing, because you indulged in trifle topics that emerged during the conversation. If this happens, you might be under the sway of drifting; if this happens quite often, you might be a drifter.

Even though the example above might not seem life-threatening, drifting can have severe consequences when important things are at stake. Imagine forgetting a critical point that cost you a significant business deal, a key relationship, etc.

The opposite of a disciplined person is a drifter. Disciplined people live their lives paying utmost attention to the things that matter, while drifters allow every kind of idea and conversation to steal their attention/focus.

# 2

# A DISCIPLINED BODY

## A Disciplined Appetite

A disciplined person must have control over his/her appetite. Your appetite can also be referred to as your *cravings*. Many people experience cravings and excuse their inability to control their cravings with the statement "I have to give my body what it is asking for." The Psalmist, in Psalms 78:18, clarified an aspect of Bible history with this statement: *"They stubbornly tested God in their hearts, demanding the foods they craved."* From this passage, we understand that one of the reasons why God punished the children of Israel in the wilderness was for insisting on eating certain foods that they craved for. Their lack of discipline in their appetite got them in trouble.

In Psalms 78, from verses 29 - 31, we begin to see how God punished them for succumbing to their illicit cravings.

They were punished by God for demanding the food they craved, over the one God was willing to give to them.

> *So they ate and were well filled, for He gave them their own desire. They were not deprived of their craving; But while their food was still in their mouths, the wrath of God came against them, and slew the stoutest of them, and struck down the choice men of Israel. (Psalms 78:29-31)*

As we explore this topic, please remember that food does not necessarily make you more or less righteous.

> *But food does not commend us to God; for neither if we eat are we the better, nor if we do not eat are we the worse." (1 Corinthians 8:8)*

This also extends to mean that, you must not allow condemnation from anyone, as you begin taking steps to disciplining your appetite (Colossians 2:16).

Disciplining your appetite does not mean starving yourself. It does not mean giving in to anorexia. Contrary to what many might think, God wants us to enjoy good things in life. He is not opposed to us eating good food. The good food God wants us to enjoy is one that is good for our body. It is one that will increase strength, longevity, etc., and not one that will cause health issues.

> *Who satisfies your mouth with good things, so that your youth is renewed like the eagle's. (Psalms 103:5)*

Having a disciplined appetite simply means eating and drinking enough of what is right, when it is right and for the right reasons.

> *"Woe to you, O land, when your king is a child, And your princes feast in the morning! Blessed are you, O land, when your king is the son of nobles, And your princes feast at the proper time— For strength and not for drunkenness!" (Ecclesiastes 10:16-17)*

The above passage embodies the principles that should be associated with a disciplined appetite. Eating happens at the proper time, and its purpose is for strength, not just to satisfy a craving.

A disciplined person does everything in accordance with a defined purpose. What is the purpose of eating? Why did God make us to need food? What is food supposed to do to our bodies? These, and many more questions will be answered in this section, as we explore what it means to have a disciplined appetite.

Rick Warren wrote a bestselling book titled "The Purpose Driven Life". The truth is, every disciplined person attaches a particular purpose to every action they take. With regards to appetite, they eat to satisfy the purpose of eating, not to satisfy their every craving.

Let us attempt to break down Ecclesiastes 10:16-17, and draw more insight from this passage of scripture.

> *"Woe to you, O land, when your king is a child, And your princes feast in the morning!" (Ecclesiastes 10:16)*

It is an unfortunate situation to be ruled by an immature person. One sign of immaturity highlighted here is when the rulers eat large quantities of food in the morning.

> *Blessed are you, O land, when your king is the son of nobles, and your princes feast at the proper time—for strength and not for drunkenness! (Ecclesiastes 10:17)*

People that are ruled by mature leaders are blessed. One sign of maturity here is not that the rulers did not feast, but that they feasted at the appropriate time. I will share my perspective regarding the right time to eat, based on my study of the Bible.

Now, let us go on a journey through the Bible to get some answers to fundamental questions about food and eating.

### The Origin of Food

The manufacturer of a product is the best source for determining the intricate details of their products. The very first mention of food in the Bible was in Genesis 1:29. In this passage, God Himself specified what He wanted His creation to eat. If God brought up the idea of food, it is wisdom to find out from Him what kind of food He expects humans to eat.

> *And God said, "See, I have given you every herb that yields seed which is on the face of all the earth, and every tree whose fruit yields seed; to you it shall be for food. (Genesis 1:29)*

According to scriptures, man was made from the dust of the ground. From Genesis 2:7, we see that, *"the Lord God formed man of the dust of the ground, and breathed into his nostrils the breath of life; and man became a living being."*

Also, according to scriptures, the plant-based food that God made came from the earth; it was not created in a laboratory.

> *Then God said, "Let the earth bring forth grass, the herb that yields seed, and the fruit tree that yields fruit according to its kind, whose seed is in itself, on the earth"; and it was so. And the earth brought forth grass, the herb that yields seed according to its kind, and the tree that yields fruit, whose seed is in itself according to its kind. And God saw that it was good. (Genesis 1:11-12)*

Since the material from which the body of man was made is connected to the ground from which food comes, we can reasonably conclude that organic food is healthier than laboratory engineered food. i.e. genetically engineered foods.

After the flood, God expanded man's diet to include animals. In Genesis 9:3-4, the Bible says that *"every moving thing that lives shall be food for you. I have given you all things, even as the green herbs. But you shall not eat flesh with its life, that is, its blood."*

From a scriptural perspective, we can see that God expects human beings to eat naturally grown plants, and naturally raised animals.

## The Right Amount of Food

The current culture encourages binging. People are encouraged to binge watch television, binge on social media, binge on drinks, food, etc. With regards to appetite, binging is what the Bible calls gluttony. Different motives encourage today's culture to advocate for binging on food. The primary motive is profit. Since the love for money has, in many cases, superseded people's love for one another; advertisements, deals, specials, all encourage people to throw caution to the wind when eating. This of course is to the benefit of the business owners at the detriment of the people eating the food.

To be disciplined in your appetite, you need to listen to your body. You should pay attention to the way your body responds to certain foods or drinks and make necessary adjustments.

Also, you need to pay attention to how much food you are taking in. Ensure that you are not compelled to eat all the food that is placed before you. A person with a disciplined appetite should not be feeling heavy after eating a meal. Heaviness is a sign that perhaps you have gone beyond the ration your body was expecting.

As mentioned earlier, eating or not eating will not make you more or less righteous. There are however other benefits for ensuring you are disciplined with your appetite.

An undisciplined appetite can lead to destruction.

> *whose end is destruction, whose god is their belly, and whose glory is in their shame—who set their mind on earthly things. (Philippians 3:19)*

An undisciplined appetite can lead a person to poverty

> *Do not mix with winebibbers, or with gluttonous eaters of meat; for the drunkard and the glutton will come to poverty, and drowsiness will clothe a man with rags. (Proverbs 23:20-21)*

The result of an undisciplined appetite can be slavery

> *All things are lawful for me, but all things are not helpful. All things are lawful for me, but I will not be brought under the power of any. (1 Corinthians 6:12)*

## The Right Time to Eat

In this section, I will not be stating the actual time we ought to eat. I will, however, be showing you scripturally, how many "main" meals we ought to have each day.

> *The eyes of all look to you, and you give them their food at the proper time. (Psalm 145:15)*

According to this scripture above, God gives His children food at the right time; we will be exploring biblical examples in a moment. In Ecclesiastes 3:1-8, we see a catalog of things that ought to be done at the proper time. Eating and drinking has to be done in its time. There is an abundance of materials on what kind of food to eat and when. Since I am not an expert in that area, I will only state biblical facts that relates to the appropriate time to eat/drink. The question now is: When is the proper time to eat and drink?

When Elijah declared a drought on the land in accordance with God's instructions, he was told to go stay by the Brook Cherith and receive food from the ravens. God had commanded the ravens to feed Elijah and he drank water from the Brook Cherith. The interesting point to note here is that God commanded the ravens to bring him food twice daily. The first meal was served in the morning, and the second in the evening, i.e. breakfast and dinner.

> *So he went and did according to the word of the Lord, for he went and stayed by the Brook Cherith, which flows into the Jordan. 6 The ravens brought him bread and meat in the morning, and bread and meat in the evening; and he drank from the brook. 7 And it happened after a while that the brook dried up, because there had been no rain in the land. (1 Kings 17:5)*

I have often said that, you ought not to build a doctrine based on a single occurrence of an incident in the Bible. Doctrines are based on sound, and related principles in scriptures that occur at least twice.

Following that principle, here is another Bible reference that points to the fact that God endorses a twice daily mealtime.

> *And the Lord spoke to Moses, saying, "I have heard the complaints of the children of Israel. Speak to them,*

*saying, 'At twilight you shall eat meat, and in the morning you shall be filled with bread. And you shall know that I am the Lord your God.'" So it was that quails came up at evening and covered the camp, and in the morning the dew lay all around the camp. And when the layer of dew lifted, there, on the surface of the wilderness, was a small round substance, as fine as frost on the ground. So when the children of Israel saw it, they said to one another, "What is it?" For they did not know what it was. And Moses said to them, "This is the bread which the Lord has given you to eat. (Exodus 16:11-15)*

From these two scriptures, we can deduce that God endorsed eating meals twice each day. These two examples are perfect, because God was the one controlling when the people were fed. It means that if God had His way, He would want us to eat our main meals twice daily.

As we close this chapter, remember that no matter the cravings you are having, learn to ask yourself these key questions before you settle down to a sumptuous meal:

Is this the best food for me right now?
Is this the best quantity of food for me to eat?
Is this the best time for me to eat?

There are many good pieces of literature that can help you understand the foods available, and help you make the right food choices. Be cautious of the authors of those materials though, as every Tom, Dick, and Harry is attempting to cash in from the billion-dollar health and fitness market.

## The Fasting Lifestyle

Fasting is going without food as a form of worship to God. Any attempt to go without food without the intention of worshipping God could be a hunger strike, or simply an attempt at weight loss.

A person with a disciplined body is able to go without food as a form of worship to God.

The Bible tells us that our belly should not be our god. The Word of God even calls these people enemies of the cross of Christ.

> *"For many walk, of whom I have told you often, and now tell you even weeping, that they are the enemies of the cross of Christ: whose end is destruction, whose god is their belly, and whose glory is in their shame— who set their mind on earthly things." (Philippians 3:18-19)*

Jesus also spoke about fasting during His earthly ministry. He said, *"when you fast..."* (Matthew 6:16-18), which means that He expects us, His disciples, to fast regularly. If it were optional, perhaps He would have said, "if you fast…"

It takes discipline to subject your body to go without food. That is why Paul said, *"I discipline my body..."* (1 Corinthians 9:27). In order to fast, the body must be subjected to functioning without food. Your stomach will scream at you like a child seeking attention. Paul disciplined his body, simply by ignoring the noise it was making as a result of not having food to process.

A key aspect of disciplining the body is fasting. You should have set times for waiting on God in fasting. It could be yearly, quarterly, monthly, or weekly. Engage in fasting as enabled by the Holy Spirit.

For more on fasting, read "The Fasting Edge" by Jentezen Franklin.

**Exercise**
A disciplined body is a body that is constantly exercised and stretched. You do not have to go to the gym every day to exercise your body.

In the days of the old and new testament saints, physical exercise was a daily and regular occurrence. The people walked long distances without the use of the modern means of transportation, as we have today. They did not have gyms to register in. They did not have all the fancy inventions we have today, but they mainly exercised from regular daily work.

We are living in a blessed time in history. There has never been a time in history with so many inventions as we have today. The quality and quantity of innovations is unprecedented. However, instead of using this to our advantage, it has made many people resign to a life of physical inactivity. Today, you even find believers with no physical disability praying to God for parking near the entrance to the mall!

No matter how long you have settled into physical inactivity, if you make a decision today to establish discipline in that area of your life, you will yield positive results. According to

Hebrews 3:15 (NLT), "*Remember what it says: "today when you hear his voice, don't harden your hearts as Israel did when they rebelled"*." Don't harden your heart.

You can start small and gradually increase the frequency and intensity as you progress. Little exercise is better than nothing. As is said, Rome wasn't built in a day, and little drops of water can eventually make an ocean.

Even though the exercise industry is currently a multi-billion-dollar industry, it does not mean that people are getting healthier and adopting healthier physical habits. Contrary to what the exercise industry's marketing machine wants you and I to believe, you do not have to register in a gym to adopt a healthy exercise routine. Any productive activity you can engage in to exercise key parts of your body counts for physical exercise. We will be exploring this in detail shortly. First, let us discuss some benefits of exercise.

**Improved Health**
Physical exercise can cause the body to produce endorphins. Endorphins are chemicals that can improve your mood; it makes you feel good about yourself and about the world around you. It is that chemical that makes you upbeat, as it is released into your body. It increases energy levels, helps to lower blood pressure, strengthens and builds bones, and it helps reduce body fat.

**Better Sleep**
Those that constantly exercise report having a good night's rest. It is often said that rest is sweet after labor. When your

body is constantly being exercised, it will maximize the benefits of sleep to recoup.

**Better Looks**

When combined with healthy eating, or even on its own, physical exercise can help a person maintain a healthy weight and look better. In fact, exercise is one of the most important parts of keeping your body at a healthy weight.

**Reduces the Risk of Certain Diseases and Helps in Aging Well**

Physical exercise can help a person age better as a result of the key aspects of the body that are exercised. A healthy heart, bones, muscles, etc. will make a person less susceptible to certain terminal illnesses (e.g. type 2 diabetes and high blood pressure), and improve the person's quality of life in old age.

In addition to all of the above, physical exercise helps to reduce stress, ward off anxiety and feelings of depression, boost self-esteem, and so on.

In conclusion, there are key parts of the body that should be regularly exercised. These include the heart (cardiovascular/aerobic exercise), bones (anaerobic exercise), joints (joint flexibility), and muscles (muscular endurance and strength). Ensure that your exercise routine is structured to consistently touch on these parts.

# 3

## DISCIPLINED EMOTIONS

### Emotional Beings

Human beings express themselves through emotions. They are also known as feelings or moods. Emotions are not necessarily bad, but as with everything else, they must be properly controlled and managed in order for one to live a successful life. There are some people we all like to associate with, because they are always upbeat, happy, etc. On the other hand, some people are always sad, depressed, and angry; smart people avoid them like a plague.

Have you ever been happy, sad, angry, disappointed, excited? Chances are, you have displayed these feelings before. Do those feelings occur automatically? Are they controllable? Can your emotions be under your control? Do you have a say in which emotions dominate you? Are you known for constantly displaying certain emotions? We will address these questions and many more in this chapter.

## Nature vs. Nurture

Every human being was created by God to display every kind of emotion. We are all able to display the emotion of joy, sadness, excitement, etc., if we choose to. In dissecting this perspective, we must understand that without doing anything extra, both nature and nurture will determine which emotions become dominant in a person's life.

## Nature

Nature refers to the emotions that naturally dominate a person's life as a result of their body composition. A person's physiological makeup determines the amount of hormones naturally secreted in their body.

A woman's physiological makeup causes her to naturally display certain emotions in comparison to a man.

Physiological makeup can make some people more prone to depression or anger. Some are more prone to be happy or excited. See the physiological makeup as the baseline that we all start with. It is the blank canvas with which we will begin this journey to emotional intelligence. Are you battling with a destructive emotion that has refused to be abated? Don't give up. Life has not dealt you a bad hand. Your starting point is simply different from others, but we can all get to the same destination of living an emotionally balanced life.

Without foraying too much into this domain, it is worthy to note that natural factors can be both man-made and God-made.

To a large extent, the physiological state of a person is determined by man-made factors. There are certain foods, chemicals, drinks, and suchlike, that a pregnant woman would consume that can alter the physiological state of their unborn child. For example, there are children that are called crack babies. These children are born, naturally addicted to certain drugs, because their mothers consumed those drugs while pregnant. These children, through no fault of theirs, may have a drastically reduced chance of living a successful life.

On the other hand, God (i.e. without any action on man's part) determines the physiological makeup of a person.

Whatever the cause, the pertinent message is that nature can determine the prevalent emotions you exhibit; you might be overly excited, or overly depressed, simply because nature played a significant role in you being the way you are. Remember, whatever your emotional starting point is, you are fearfully and wonderfully made.

> *I will praise You, for I am fearfully and wonderfully made; Marvelous are Your works, and that my soul knows very well. (Psalms 139:14)*

Even though you were transported to the earth through your mother's womb, remember that it is God that formed you. If He released you from the "factory", it simply means that He knows you are well prepared to fully function on the earth and succeed. God's words to Jeremiah gives us an insight into this. God said He formed Jeremiah while in his mother's womb. Wow! Your mother did not form you, God did. And everything God creates is very good.

> *"Before I formed you in the womb I knew you; Before you were born I sanctified you; I ordained you a prophet to the nations." (Jeremiah 1:5)*

## Nurture

On the other end of the spectrum, the way we were nurtured plays a significant role in which emotions become dominant in us.

Nurture also refers to the influences from the environment we grew up in. The parenting style we were exposed to, influences from schools, books, movies, societal culture, to mention but a few, all add up in molding our emotional disposition.

For example, a child that grew up in a home where joy was frowned upon might find it easier to frown or maintain a mild, laissez-faire attitude. In some homes, a smile, and greetings attracts a response of "what is good about the morning?" Continually hearing this could subconsciously condition a person to only display certain types of emotion.

Physical, mental, or emotional exposure to an abusive environment, especially in the formative years of a person's life, will typically lead to a person displaying more destructive emotions such as anger and depression. On the other hand, exposure to a loving environment in the formative years of a person's life could also lead to a person displaying healthier emotions such as joy.

We do not get to choose which homes we get born into, just like we don't get to choose most of the natural factors that can influence our emotions. Whatever your environment might have sown into you, remember that God can turn things around for you. Even though your environment has sown lethal emotional seeds into you, God can still turn things around for you. Quit questioning God. That is an easy route, and most people take that route. It absolves them of any responsibility, and is not a sign of maturity. Instead, begin to ask the question, "what must I do to develop the right emotions?"

Do you know that Joseph in the Bible was born into an emotionally toxic environment? His father was swindled into marrying Joseph's aunt. There was open rivalry between his mother and his aunt. Envy, backbiting, and all sorts of evil things were present in that family. Joseph's dad complicated matters by openly displaying his love for Joseph at the expense of his siblings. As a result, Joseph's brothers sold him into slavery, after they had unreservedly contemplated to kill him. Despite all these, Joseph was still able to trust in God, and love his brothers and family. It might seem like a daunting task, but we can do all things through Christ who strengthens us (Philippians 4:13). Your story might be worse than Joseph's, but if you put your trust in the same God that Joseph put his trust in, you'll come out on top.

## Good vs. Bad Emotions

God gave us all emotions to enjoy life with. Emotions can make life more colorful. Many people, however, believe that some emotions are better than others. Yes, some emotions can destroy your life, while others can help build it. However, that does not mean some emotions are bad, while others are good. Join me on a journey through the Bible to see examples where God displayed several emotions and emotional responses, which He also deposited in man.

> **Joy** – *In that hour Jesus rejoiced in the Spirit and said, "I thank You, Father, Lord of heaven and earth, that You have hidden these things from the wise and prudent and revealed them to babes. Even so, Father, for so it seemed good in Your sight. (Luke 10:21)*
>
> **Laughter** – *He who sits in the heavens shall laugh; The Lord shall hold them in derision. (Psalms 2:4)*
>
> **Tears** – *Jesus wept. (John 11:35)*
>
> **Regret** – *And the Lord regretted that He had made man on the earth, and He was grieved at heart. (Genesis 6:6 AMPC)*
>
> **Anger** – *And the LORD said to Moses, "I have seen this people, and indeed it is a stiff-necked people! Now therefore, let Me alone, that My wrath may burn hot against them and I may consume them. And I will make of you a great nation." (Exodus 32:9-10)*
>
> **Love** – *Then the Jews said, "See how He loved him!" (John 11:36)*

As you can see, our Father in heaven is emotionally mature to display a variety of emotions when necessary. The problem isn't that some emotions are good or bad. The issue is that most people are not in control of their emotions, rather, their emotions are controlling them. We should not be captive to our own emotions. We should be able to decide our emotional response without being enslaved to them.

For example, many people are of the opinion that anger is a sin. Many believe that they must never be angry. Wouldn't that make God an unrighteous judge? If He displayed anger, wouldn't it be hypocrisy for Him to say we couldn't get angry? The bible doesn't say that we shouldn't get angry. Is that a surprise? Let the Bible speak for itself.

> *"Be angry, and do not sin": do not let the sun go down on your wrath. (Ephesians 4:26)*
> *Idolatry, sorcery, hatred, contentions, jealousies, outbursts of wrath, selfish ambitions, dissensions, heresies. (Galatians 5:20)*
> *Do not hasten in your spirit to be angry, For anger rests in the bosom of fools. (Ecclesiastes 7:9)*

The Bible frowns against uncontrollable anger. It also frowns against an outburst of anger. There are times when anger must be displayed, but it must be under the control of the Holy Spirit in you.

The next section of this chapter will be devoted to how we can discipline our emotions.

## Our Emotional Response is a Choice

The very first sin that mankind committed was the sin of disobedience to God. Adam succumbed to his wife's suggestion to eat the fruit of the *"tree of the knowledge of good and evil"* (Genesis 3:6), which was in the midst of the Garden of Eden. The interesting point is that God could have forgiven Adam, if he repented and asked for forgiveness. Instead, he chose to absolve himself from the responsibility of his choice, by blaming his wife. God wasn't pleased with that. Likewise, we humans can choose our emotional response, instead of blaming people, when we indeed have the absolute power to choose a response.

Every human being is able to choose the kind of emotions they will succumb to, either consciously or subconsciously. You can either generate the emotions yourself, or put yourself in situations where those emotions can be generated. For example, choosing to watch a comedy show instead of remaining sad and in bed all day, or choosing to put an end to an abusive relationship to maintain your sanity.

Let's put this idea into practice right away! Now, begin to laugh. Yes, I am serious. Laugh for the next two minutes! I don't mean chuckle. Do you see that you can choose which emotion to display? Now, you may be thinking, that is being fake; I want to be real. I only laugh when something is genuinely funny. I only cry when something is genuinely sad. Is that really true? We all watch movies that we know are fabricated, but they still elicit emotions from us. If you can laugh to a made-up story, is it odd for you to laugh or smile (on your own) for no apparent reason? Or at least, laugh for any reason of your choosing? You could even remember a funny experience and respond to it by laughing.

## Choosing the Right Emotional Response

The first step to take is to determine what kind of emotions you desire to be the norm in your life. Do you want to be a joyful person or a sad person? Do you want to be an angry person or a loving person? Make that decision right now!

Boldly declare these confessions:

> I am a loving person.
> I am a joyful person.
> I am enjoying peace.
> I am in control of my emotional response to every event.
> I laugh when I need to laugh.
> I cry when I need to cry.
> I am unashamed of my emotional response.
> I am not held captive by anyone's expectations of my emotional response.

Remember that no emotion is good or bad. Yes, some emotions can set you back, while others can propel you forward. The message being conveyed through this book is that, you decide what kind of dominant emotions you want to be a part of your life, and deliberately structure your life to achieve them.

Stop and think about it; If man were unable to choose his emotional response, why would God hold him accountable for his actions?

Now that you have consciously decided which emotions you want to dominate you, you can now begin to take steps every day in line with that decision.

Now, genuinely answer the following questions:

> What do I need to do each day to generate the kind of emotions I desire?
> What habits do I need to eliminate from my life, in order to generate the kind of emotions I desire?
> What kind of people do I need to associate with, in order to generate the kind of emotions I desire?
> Who do I need to cut off ties with, in order to generate the kind of emotions I desire?

In order for this to be effective, I recommend approaching it from three perspectives: spiritual, mental, and physical. All perspectives are important and must be given appropriate attention.

### The spiritual perspective

Having a daily prayer life.

Studying the Bible (the word of God) daily.

Meditating on the Bible daily.

Actively remaining under a God-ordained spiritual authority.

### The mental perspective

Listening to anointed (and uplifting) music.

Meditating only on thoughts that have passed the test of Philippians 4:8, i.e. truthful, noble, just, pure, lovely, good report, virtuous, and praiseworthy. (More on this in the next chapter)

Keeping a record of things, you are thankful for and regularly reviewing it.

## The physical perspective

Eating nourishing foods.

Exercising different parts of your body (as discussed in Chapter 1).

Visiting your doctor to determine your minerals and vitamins deficiency, and taking appropriate multivitamins to remedy deficiencies.

The above is by no means exhaustive, but I believe this will move you in the right direction. As you practice the recommendations above, I believe that you will record progress, which will encourage you to keep forging ahead. You can do it! Remember that according to Philippians 4:13, *"I can do all things through Christ who strengthens me."*

## Divine Dominant Emotional Expectations

As mentioned earlier, we are able to choose our emotional responses.

No emotion is good or bad. Some emotions, if dominant, can destroy a person's life, while some can lead a person to success.

> *For you, brethren, have been called to liberty; only do not use liberty as an opportunity for the flesh, but through love serve one another. For all the law is fulfilled in one*

> *word, even in this: "You shall love your neighbor as your-*
> *self." But if you bite and devour one another, beware lest*
> *you be consumed by one another! (Galatians 5:13-15)*

What are the dominant emotions that will lead to success in a person's life? Galatians 5:22-23 gives us the answer to that question.

> *But the fruit of the Spirit is love, joy, peace, longsuffer-*
> *ing, kindness, goodness, faithfulness, gentleness, self-con-*
> *trol. Against such there is no law. (Galatians 5:22-23)*

God expects His children to strive daily to walk in these emotional traits. The reason this topic is in this book is so that these emotional responses can be practiced.

**Love**
The Word of God makes it clear that God is love.

> *Beloved, let us love one another, for love is of God; and*
> *everyone who loves is born of God and knows God. He*
> *who does not love does not know God, for God is love.*
> *(1 John 4:7-8)*

God's definition of love is different from the love that society advocates. Jesus told many parables to help us understand the God kind of love. One of those parables is about a father and his two sons (Luke 15:11-32). There are a few lessons from this love parable.

Why did the father allow the son to leave with his inheritance? In fact, why did the father give the inheritance to the son in the first place? True love does not manipulate others into doing what they want.

God knows that when many of His children become independent, they will no longer depend on Him. He knows that when many of them get the job, spouse, children, and/or money they seek, they will no longer be committed to Him, as they were initially. Nevertheless, He still grants their hearts' desires, somewhat hoping they will continue to serve Him and make the choice to depend on Him.

God's love is a kind of love that gives people, who are mature and mentally sound enough, the opportunity to make a decision they believe is good for them, even though God knows it may not be the best.

God's love is a kind of love that allows a person that is old enough, wise enough, and capable of making decisions, to determine what they want to do, and that decision is respected.

The prodigal son's father did not troll him on Facebook or follow him to the country he went to, in the name of love. But when the son came back home himself, he was ready to receive him.

God's kind of love respects mature people's decisions.

The Bible never said that the father went after the son and begged, or ordered him to come back home when he saw he had ran out of money.

God's love restores.
God's love transforms.

God's love forgives.
God's love looks for opportunities to give.
God's love receives.
God's love covers shame.

When we ask God for forgiveness, there are only three categories of people that still bring up what happened in the past. They are: you, others, and the devil.

## Joy

Joy can be defined as the emotion of great happiness; it is also known as gladness. Many do not take responsibility for their own emotions, and joy is not an exception. You do not need to wait for an exceptional event before you become joyful.

In every seemingly negative situation, always ask yourself this question: how can I make the best of this situation, to be and to do all God has called me to be and do?

> *Though the fig tree may not blossom, Nor fruit be on the vines; Though the labor of the olive may fail, And the fields yield no food; Though the flock may be cut off from the fold, And there be no herd in the stalls—* **Yet I will rejoice in the LORD, I will joy in the God of my salvation.** *The LORD God is my strength; He will make my feet like deer's feet, And He will make me walk on my high hills. (Habakkuk 3:17-19)*

## Peace

This can be defined as being balanced. It is being in a state of equilibrium. Peace is the absence of worry, anxiety, and concerns. It is being in a state of calmness, where the mind is not clogged up.

> *And the peace of God, which surpasses all understanding, will guard your hearts and minds through Christ Jesus. (Philippians 4:7)*
> *And let the peace of God rule in your hearts, to which also you were called in one body; and be thankful. (Colossians 3:15)*

What are the emotional traits that should not be dominant in a person's life?

## Outbursts of Anger

The emotion of anger is not a sin. God knows that we will experience situations that will make us angry, and His word never says that we should not be angry. It is unhealthy, however, for a person to always be angry. It is not a valid excuse that you are always angry because people are always getting you angry.

Below are the guidelines we are given concerning anger.

The sun must not go down on your anger. You can sometimes be angry but not sin.

> *"Be angry, and do not sin": do not let the sun go down on your wrath. (Ephesians 4:26)*

Avoid the outburst of wrath. Those that practice this will not inherit the kingdom of God.

> *Now the works of the flesh are evident, which are: adultery, fornication, uncleanness, lewdness, idolatry, sorcery, hatred, contentions, jealousies, outbursts of wrath, selfish ambitions, dissensions, heresies, envy, murders, drunkenness, revelries, and the like; of which I tell you beforehand, just as I also told you in time past, that those who practice such things will not inherit the kingdom of God. (Galatians 5:19-21)*

Jesus displayed what seemed like the emotion of anger when He chased out the money changers from the Synagogue, but He was not out of control while doing it. The Bible called this zeal. He passionately displayed His love for God by driving out those that desecrated the temple — by turning the temple into a marketplace.

> *Now the Passover of the Jews was at hand, and Jesus went up to Jerusalem. And He found in the temple those who sold oxen and sheep and doves, and the money changers doing business. When He had made a whip of cords, He drove them all out of the temple, with the sheep and the oxen, and poured out the changers' money and overturned the tables. And He said to those who sold doves, "Take these things away! Do not make My Father's house a house of merchandise!" Then*

*His disciples remembered that it was written, "Zeal for Your house has eaten Me up." So the Jews answered and said to Him, "What sign do You show to us, since You do these things?" (John 2:13-18)*

It becomes a sin when the emotion of anger begins to control you, instead of your spirit, under the leading of the Holy Spirit, being in control.

## Prolonged Sadness

Sadness is another emotion that God expects us to experience.
God says we should mourn with those who are mourning.

*Rejoice with those who rejoice, and weep with those who weep. (Romans 12:15)*

When Moses died, God told the children of Israel to mourn his death. He, however, did not tell them to mourn forever. He told them how long to mourn for.

The emotion of sadness breeds negative consequences when it is experienced for a prolonged period. How long is prolonged? God told the children of Israel how long to mourn for.

*And the children of Israel wept for Moses in the plains of Moab thirty days. So the days of weeping and mourning for Moses ended. (Deuteronomy 34:8)*

We cannot experience compassion without experiencing sorrow. Another way to understand compassion is to see it as empathy, or putting yourself in another person's shoes. It also means feeling what the other person is feeling.

> *For we do not have a High Priest who cannot sympathize with our weaknesses, but was in all points tempted as we are, yet without sin. (Hebrews 4:15)*

Prolonged sorrow can lead to depression and other health-related issues. It should be avoided at all costs.

## Disappointment

Disappointment is when we feel let down, when we feel abandoned by someone, or when we get an unfavorable outcome from an event. Disappointment always happens when we have wrong expectations—either of people or of events. The Holy Spirit taught me that wrong expectations will always lead to disappointment.

The solution to never feeling disappointed is NOT to avoid having any expectations at all. Having no expectations of people or events might sound good, but the effects can be far-reaching.

Without expectation, a.k.a. hope, we cannot have faith. And since faith in God is the bedrock of Christianity, any solution that suggests we do away with our expectations of people or events is a dangerous proposition.

Instead, the solution to avoiding disappointment is to have the right expectation.

***Expectation of people*** – always remember that only God is infallible. No matter how good or noble people's intentions are, they can fail us. This is because no human being is in control of every extenuating factor. There are several things that can make a person unable to meet their commitments, even though they sincerely planned to.

When dealing with people, keep their track record in mind. If there has been a series of disappointments from this person, it is not unfair to expect they can disappoint you again. Many Christians mistake this for forgiving and forgetting. They erroneously avoid considering a person's track record, for fear of appearing not to have forgiven their previous wrongs. For example, if a friend failed to pay back a loan because of circumstances within their control, God still expects you to forgive him/her. When this same friend comes back again for another loan, it is wisdom to consider their track record in your decision-making process. It will be unwise to lend that friend money again, if you're not convinced that they will pay back the loan this time.

***Expectation of events*** – another source of disappointment is when a person expects an event to unfold in a particular way and it doesn't. For example, you might have prayed for a sick loved one, expecting them to be healed according to the word of God, but they still passed on to glory. Like I mentioned earlier, if you choose not to have an expectation, you'll not have faith.

The correct approach in this situation is to get the truth concerning the outcome of every event. If it is an event that the Bible directly speaks about, align your expectation with the predicted outcome from the Bible. For example, if the Bible says, "*with long life will I satisfy you and show you my salvation*"

(Psalms 91:16), it will be wise for you to expect long life; so long as you follow the instructions attached to that promise in scriptures. In cases where you believe that you followed the instructions, but the outcome did not match your expectation; instead of being disappointed, go ask those directly responsible for the outcome why it turned out that way.

For example, I was involved in praying for the healing of the mother of one of my spiritual sons. We prayed in faith, we anointed with oil, we did all that we knew the Bible expected us to do. On a particular day, I saw a vision of her passing on to glory. Because that was not my expectation, I rebuked the vision and declared it wasn't coming to pass. Sadly, she still passed on to glory. Instead of beating myself up over it and allowing it to take me down the abyss of disappointment, I went to God in prayer and asked Him why this happened. His answer to me was that she made up her mind to go, because of the intensity of the pain. She tried to hold on as long as she could, but the pain became unbearable. Even though she could have been healed by God, the process and pace of the healing was too slow. We have to understand that only God has the full picture at all times. He went on to explain that no matter how much you pray for a person, if they are old enough and sane enough to make a decision, you cannot use your prayers to override their decision/will. One exception to this rule is if the person has given you authority over them. Understanding this helped me avoid disappointment and the thought that my prayer was ineffective.

Even John the Baptist got disappointed. In the beginning of his ministry, he boldly declared that Jesus was the savior

(John 1:29-34). When he got imprisoned and perhaps Jesus (his cousin) did not come to rescue him, he began to doubt that Jesus was the savior. The outcome of this event made him disappointed, to the extent of sending his disciples to confirm again from Jesus if He was truly the savior.

> *Then the disciples of John reported to him concerning all these things. And John, calling two of his disciples to him, sent them to Jesus, saying, "Are You the Coming One, or do we look for another?" When the men had come to Him, they said, "John the Baptist has sent us to You, saying, 'Are You the Coming One, or do we look for another?'" And that very hour He cured many of infirmities, afflictions, and evil spirits; and to many blind He gave sight. Jesus answered and said to them, "Go and tell John the things you have seen and heard: that the blind see, the lame walk, the lepers are cleansed, the deaf hear, the dead are raised, the poor have the gospel preached to them. And blessed is he who is not offended because of Me." (Luke 7:18-23)*

## Discouragement

This can occur when something does not happen soon enough, or in the manner we desire. Discouragement will leave a person less hopeful or enthusiastic. Discouragement and disappointment can lead to similar outcomes. David and his men were discouraged when their wives and children were captured in Ziklag

*Now it happened, when David and his men came to Ziklag, on the third day, that the Amalekites had invaded the South and Ziklag, attacked Ziklag and burned it with fire, and had taken captive the women and those who were there, from small to great; they did not kill anyone, but carried them away and went their way. So David and his men came to the city, and there it was, burned with fire; and their wives, their sons, and their daughters had been taken captive. Then David and the people who were with him lifted up their voices and wept, until they had no more power to weep. And David's two wives, Ahinoam the Jezreelitess, and Abigail the widow of Nabal the Carmelite, had been taken captive. Now David was greatly distressed, for the people spoke of stoning him, because the soul of all the people was grieved, every man for his sons and his daughters. But David strengthened himself in the LORD his God. (1 Samuel 30:1-6)*

David's response to that event is one of the most powerful ways to deal with discouragement. The Bible says, "*David strengthened himself in the Lord*" (1 Samuel 30:6). To my knowledge, discouragement is something that cannot be prevented, but it can be appropriately responded to, when it happens. Being sensitive enough to detect that an event could get you discouraged, and responding appropriately is crucial in dealing with discouragement.

## Irritation

This is an intense uncomfortable feeling (mental, physical, or emotional uneasiness), or distress. This can happen when we are out of our comfort zone. We can be irritated when what we see, hear, feel, smell, taste is not what we are comfortable with.

> *And it came to pass, when she pestered him daily with her words and pressed him, so that his soul was vexed to death. (Judges 16:16)*

## Fear

This is a state of being afraid. This is an emotion that we all experience; however, we don't all respond to it in the same way. We experience it at different levels of frequency and intensity. God knows that we are human beings, and that we can experience fear. That is why the first thing angels say when they appear to a human being is fear not.

> *And when Zacharias saw him, he was troubled, and fear fell upon him. But the angel said to him, "Do not be afraid, Zacharias, for your prayer is heard; and your wife Elizabeth will bear you a son, and you shall call his name John. (Luke 1:12-13)*
> *Now in the sixth month the angel Gabriel was sent by God to a city of Galilee named Nazareth, to a virgin betrothed to a man whose name was Joseph, of the house of David. The virgin's name was Mary. And having come in, the angel said to her, "Rejoice, highly favored one, the Lord is with you; blessed are you among women!"*

*But when she saw him, she was troubled at his saying, and considered what manner of greeting this was. Then the angel said to her, "Do not be afraid, Mary, for you have found favor with God. (Luke 1:26-30)*

If the angels told them to fear not, it means that we can make a decision not to be afraid. We can choose not to respond in fear. You can choose not to allow the emotion of fear to take over you. According to scriptures, we have not been given the spirit of fear, but of power, love, and of a sound mind (2 Timothy 1:7). The emotion of fear can easily metamorphose into oppression by the spirit of fear, if care is not taken. Fear is not to be tolerated. The emotion of fear can limit a person, among other things. You have the power to defeat fear. If you are born-again, i.e. accepted Jesus into your heart as your Lord and Savior, you have the power to overcome fear. If you are currently bound by fear, confidently declare this prayer after me:

> **"In the name of Jesus Christ of Nazareth, I rebuke every spirit of fear that is dominating my life. From this day, I am free and free indeed."**

### Anxiety

This is similar to fear, but is not quite fear. Anxiety is a heightened state of anticipation about something—either positive or negative. This means that anxiety can be developed for good things as well as bad things: we could be anxious from expecting a new car to arrive, and we could be anxious from hoping a relative survives an operation. The Bible gives us good advice concerning this.

> *Be anxious for nothing, but in everything by prayer and supplication, with thanksgiving, let your requests be made known to God. (Philippians 4:6)*

With a disciplined emotion, you can make your emotions work for you in fulfilling your destiny. Remember, I am not advocating you deceive and manipulate people with your emotions. Rather, I am advocating the application of self-discipline to your emotional life, which would enable you to be lifted up, and not brought down; to be a success and not a failure; to be a winner in life and not a loser; furthermore, to obtain favor and not be rejected.

See you at the top!

# 4

# A DISCIPLINED MIND

## The Mind

The mind is that part of the human body that does these three major things: receives information, processes information, and stores information. The better the ability of a mind to do these things will determine how sound that mind is. The mind also generates output that is communicated in different forms like speaking, writing, etc.

Just as the body can be kept healthy in several ways, the mind can also be kept healthy by what it is constantly fed with, the way it is exercised, and so on.

The mind is like a factory. A well-functioning factory excels in its ability to get the right raw materials in, at the right time; convert those raw materials into finished goods; store the finished goods; and finally, ensure that those finished goods reach their customers in a timely manner.

Everyone that God created has a mind. The mind resides in the soul of everyone. The soul is made up of the emotions, mind (or intellect), and will. Even though every human has a mind, each person's mind, however, functions at different levels and could be affected by several factors: genetics, upbringing, level of exercise, etc. This book is focused on how a person can improve the functioning of their mind, by applying basic discipline to it. Remember, applying discipline to something good makes it better. Applying discipline to something better will make it the best.

The Bible talks a lot about the mind of a person. How we make use of this treasure, the mind, can determine the direction of a person's life. It can affect their relationship with the Godhead, with others, and their overall success in life. In essence, the way you use your mind can mean the difference between being free and being subjugated.

It is clear from history that the civilizations that dominated others did so because they were more disciplined and developed mentally. Does this mean that the subjugated civilizations were not mentally developed? Absolutely not! I do believe, however, that the subjugated ones had developed minds, but perhaps in areas that were not essentially relevant. An ancient proverb says, "it does not matter how fast you are going, if you're headed in the wrong direction."

A disciplined mind is a priceless treasure. Successful organizations are trading on their treasure trove of highly disciplined minds that are brought together to achieve specific organizational goals.

If you desire a sound and disciplined mind, expect God to release that grace to you as you read this chapter. Open your heart to the words in the pages of this book, as I join my faith with yours, so that your life will be transformed.

I believe these words from the Bible; God has given us a sound mind.

> *For God has not given us a spirit of fear, but of power and of love and of a sound mind. (2 Timothy 1:7)*

The Bible tells us to be transformed by renewing our minds (Romans 12:2). This chapter will show you how to renew, or in other words, further discipline your mind.

As I mentioned earlier, the mind receives information. Let us explore this function of the mind, and how to discipline it.

## Receiving Information

### Characteristics of High Quality Information

Have you heard the saying "garbage in, garbage out"? This saying applies very much to the mind. If you feed it with trash, it will process trash, and eventually produce trash. The mind is disciplined by ensuring that the information it is fed with is consistently of high quality. According to Philippians 4:8, high quality information must have the following eight characteristics: true, noble, just, pure, lovely, good report, virtue and praiseworthy.

> *Finally, brethren, whatever things are true, whatever things are noble, whatever things are just, whatever*

*things are pure, whatever things are lovely, whatever things are of good report, if there is any virtue and if there is anything praiseworthy—meditate on these things. (Philippians 4:8)*

## True

The definition of truth has been viciously attacked in every generation. In this generation, false mass media reports, otherwise known as "fake news", have risen to prominence as a result of the mass adoption of the internet. Many malicious characters have unleashed a slew of misinformation.

Truth and fact differ considerably. Fact is information that can be proven scientifically. Truth on the other hand transcends science. Truth is the highest order of information. Truth is greater than fact, because truth can always change fact. Given this definition of truth, it means that the source of truth has to transcend the human race.

Truth can only come from God. That is why Jesus said that He alone is the way, the truth, and the life (John 14:6). This means that only God's word is truth. Therefore, what is truth? It is the words that originate from God. This means that any information that did not originate from God can never be truth. At best, it can be a fact, which as I mentioned earlier, is lower in power and quality than the truth.

The very definition of a miracle, sign, or wonder, is the truth triumphing over the fact. God's word can change any fact, even if that fact has been scientifically proven. Here are a few examples from the Bible.

### *Lazarus was raised from the dead*
In John 11, the Bible tells a story about the death of a man called Lazarus. The fact was that Lazarus died (John 11:14, 17, 34, 38, 39). The truth, however, was in the words that Jesus spoke in John 11:11. Jesus said He was going to wake Lazarus up from his "sleep". Those words that Jesus spoke effectively changed Lazarus' state from "dead" to "asleep". And since truth transcends fact, Lazarus eventually came back alive in line with Jesus' words (John 11:44).

### *Elijah and the Widow of Zarephath*
In 1 Kings 17:8-16, we see an account of Elijah and the Widow in Zarephath. When Elijah met the widow, she was almost running out of food for her and her family (v. 12). This was the fact, and could be easily proven by observation. Elijah, however, declared the word of the Lord to the Widow, Elijah declared the truth (v. 14). As a result of the truth that was declared and believed, the fact was turned around to line up with the truth (v. 15-16).

In John 18:37-38, we see an interesting dialogue between Pontius Pilate, and Jesus Christ. Pilate was asking the same question that many people are asking today. Pilate asked a rhetorical question, "What is truth?"

Jesus gives us that answer. God's word is truth. In His prayer to God the Father, Jesus said, "*Sanctify them by Your truth. Your word is truth*" (John 17:17).

You must ensure that the words you allow access into your mind are the truth and nothing but the truth. If you allow garbage into your mind, your mind will process the garbage, produce the garbage, and as a result, turn your life into garbage.

Before you begin to process any information, adopt the discipline of consistently asking yourself the question "Is this true?" In essence, ask yourself "does God's word agree with this information?" If the answer is no, discard the information, regardless of the source. If the answer is yes, accept the information, regardless of you or others' opinion.

For example, if when watching a movie, you come across a scene that is causing you to be afraid, ask yourself if that scene is actually true. Of course, the answer is no! Part of the issue in the world today is that many people have brought scenes from fiction into their reality. They have read and watched well laid out plots, and have allowed those stories into their mind and began to create realities based on them. The result of this is a confused life.

The next time you are tempted to bring a fictional story into your mind for processing, remember to tell yourself to stop!!! That is only fiction. It is not true. Be entertained but don't bring it into reality.

## Noble

The next characteristics of high quality information is nobility. Nobility means something that is worthy of reverence, and is honorable and worthy of respect.

Thoughts related to low self-esteem do not fit this criterion. Noble thoughts are not thoughts of pride, but rather, thoughts in line with the picture of who we are from the word of God. For example, the Bible says we are fearfully and wonderfully made (Psalms 139:14). Thinking along these lines are noble thoughts.

Noble thoughts are thoughts in line with our exalted position in Christ. They are honorable thoughts about ourselves, others and situations.

Noble thoughts are humble thoughts. If a thought comes to your mind that you are the greatest of all the people God ever made, it should not be accepted into the mind's processor, as this can lead to pride and error. Lowliness of mind is another way to describe nobility.

> *Let nothing be done through selfish ambition or conceit, but in lowliness of mind let each esteem others better than himself. (Philippians 2:3)*

Any information, regardless of the source, contrary to our nobility must not be accepted into the mind for processing. The Bible gives us an example to follow.

> *Let this mind be in you which was also in Christ Jesus, who, being in the form of God, did not consider it robbery to be equal with God, but made Himself of no reputation, taking the form of a bondservant, and coming in the likeness of men. (Philippians 2:5-7)*

Verse 5 above can be re-written as *"allow this kind of thought into your minds, because Christ Jesus accepted this into his mind."* In other words, Jesus allowed the thoughts of His covenant position as part of the Godhead to persist in His mind.

## Just

This relates to the kinds of thoughts that are ethically right. They are thoughts that are proper, and fair to those involved. It is free from favoritism, self-interest, and bias.

An example will be to avoid thoughts of racism, discrimination, tribalism, etc. This is particularly critical to note in this time we are presently living in, because of the prejudice that is common in the world. Most media outlets have known pre-established biases. They are constantly reporting on issues in a way that reinforces the views that they have.

Another example is not meditating on negative words passed on to us, about people whom we have never met. It is not fair on the person being castigated that someone else had already made up their mind (i.e. a negative view) about them, before even giving them a benefit of doubt.

## Pure

Truth that is shared with the wrong motive is impure. For example, the devil used the truth, i.e. God's word, to tempt Jesus. The scriptures the devil quoted were true, but because his motive was to steal, kill, and destroy Christ, it was not pure, and hence Jesus had to discard it.

Pure information is therefore information that is true and coming from a genuine motive. God wants us to meditate on pure thoughts.

## Lovely

Lovely things inspire you to love. The media is structured to disseminate negative information, or not-so-good news. Let's face it, if all they reported were love-filled messages, most people will not patronize the news media. Keeping this in mind, you will have to consciously go searching for lovely information to meditate on by yourself.

In all we do, we have to be properly balanced. I am not advocating that you walk around as a blindly optimistic person. You have to see the good and evil in the world that we live in. God does the same. All I am advocating, based on scripture, is that even though you are fully aware of the evil in the world, you are not meant to keep thinking about it all day long. We are not meant to preoccupy ourselves with those kinds of thoughts. No matter the evil in the world, there are still good things happening. Yes, someone was unjustly killed by police. On the other hand, the Spirit of God is moving, and thousands of people are being saved in single meetings. The kind of revival we are experiencing in this time is unprecedented in all of history, even unknown in bible times. You will have to choose whether you will preoccupy your thoughts with lovely things or otherwise.

## Good Report

What is a good report? It is good news. A good report simply means a testimony. Thinking about testimonies is refreshing.

> *As cold water to a weary soul, so is good news from a far country. (Proverbs 25:25)*

It boosts your faith and causes you to be more grateful, among other things. Is your faith shaking? Are you beginning to doubt whether God can come through for you? Instead of allowing thoughts of worry and anxiety, think about testimonies.

A resume is a report of a person's past performances that gives an employer an indication of whether the person is a viable candidate or not. Did you know that meditating on testimonies is the equivalent of reading God's resume? Imagine what your faith will look like, when you meditate on the testimony of the Red Sea parting for the Israelites to go through. If you truly keep testimonies in your heart, it will be difficult for your faith to fail.

There are so many good reports all around us. There are many testimonies of divine protection, provision, favor, healing, etc., all around us. We have to train our information taste buds to appreciate them. Document your testimonies. Write down other people's striking testimonies. In addition to the testimonies in the Bible, our testimonies and that of others should be readily available for us to meditate on.

## Virtuous

Virtuous is an adjective from the noun virtue. Virtue simply means something that is chaste, impeccable, innocent, righteous, sinless, and so on. In essence, every good character trait can be classified as a virtue. This implies that every other virtue that was not listed in Philippians 4:8 is also inclusive.

## Praiseworthy

Something praiseworthy is one that is exciting and brings gladness. It is the kind of news that will cause you to glorify

God in heaven. Testimonies also have this kind of effect on a person. It sometimes leaves you speechless and just saying "wow, God is good". Can you imagine making it your lifestyle to meditate on praiseworthy things? You will always be filled with joy.

## Trustworthy Sources of Sound Information

There are superfoods that contain lots of nutrients that are good for the body. In the same way, there are some super-sources of information that contains needed nutrients for a healthy mind. If you discipline yourself to consume healthy doses of them on a regular basis, you will enjoy a sound spirit and soul. These superfoods are the Word of God (the Bible and personal revelations He gives to you), testimonies and Holy Spirit inspired materials.

## Position Yourself to Learn

A disciplined mind is one that is able to receive the right kind of information and do the right thing with that information.

Wisdom is defined as the correct application of knowledge. Knowledge is information. Every human being has knowledge built up inside of them. It started subconsciously from birth, and continues until death. Knowledge is so vital; it is a major pillar behind successful people.

Learning is not simply reading a book, listening to a message, etc. It goes beyond that. Learning starts from the heart, and the way we are positioned.

Have you ever asked yourself what happens when a person is learning? A few things happen.

The ideal learning process is like dishwashing, and the learner is the dish. We go through a process of course correction; a process where wrong assertions are corrected.

> *You are already clean because of the word which I have spoken to you. (John 15:3)*

The ideal learning process is like cooking. The learner is the cooked food. Several key points from the learning session merges with our experience and the state of our heart, which leaves us better than we were in the beginning. Peter and John did not go to traditional schools. They were schooled by Jesus, and "cooked" to become bold informed men.

> *Now when they saw the boldness of Peter and John, and perceived that they were uneducated and untrained men, they marveled. And they realized that they had been with Jesus. (Acts 4:13)*

## Humility

A proud person cannot learn from someone else. They usually claim they can only learn from God. The foremost position to assume is that of humility.

In this context, we can define humility as accepting that though you know, you do not know enough, and still need to learn more.

> *And if anyone thinks that he knows anything, he knows nothing yet as he ought to know. (1 Corinthians 8:2)*

Humility is assuming the position that though you know certain things, some of those things might be insufficient or untrue; hence you are willing to shift your position, i.e. to be convinced, if sufficient proof is provided.

> *At that time a Jew named Apollos came to Ephesus. He was an educated man from Alexandria. He knew the Scriptures very well. Apollos had been taught the way of the Lord. He spoke with great power. He taught the truth about Jesus. But he only knew about John's baptism. He began to speak boldly in the synagogue. Priscilla and Aquila heard him. So they invited him to their home. There they gave him a better understanding of the way of God. Apollos wanted to go to Achaia. The brothers and sisters agreed with him. They wrote to the believers there. They asked them to welcome him. When he arrived, he was a great help to those who had become believers by God's grace. In public meetings, he argued strongly against Jews who disagreed with him. He proved from the Scriptures that Jesus was the Messiah. (Acts 18:24-28)*

I love the story in the scripture above because many people equate humility with foolishness. This is a wrong comparison. A humble person is not a foolish person. Apollos was already very knowledgeable before he encountered Priscilla and Aquila. He, however, displayed humility when he allowed himself to be tutored by more experienced believers. Is it not amazing that the Bible acknowledged that Apollos already spoke with great power? Yet Priscilla and Aquila saw the gaps in his understanding, and proceeded to mentor him. No matter how much you know, there is more to learn.

Sometimes, you might know enough for your current level, but in order to proceed to a higher level, you need to humble yourself to learn from others.

Before any learning session, position yourself humbly as a receiver. Say this aloud: "**I declare that I am humble. The humility of Jesus is upon my life. I can learn from whoever I need to learn from, in order to be and do what God has called me to be and do.**"

When you are learning from others, ask questions to enhance your understanding of what they are communicating, and not what you are thinking. Don't seek to verify your knowledge when you hear others speak; instead, seek to understand what they are saying. Seek to understand the concepts they are communicating, before you arrive at the conclusion that they are wrong.

Until you humble yourself, God will not give you access to understand His secrets. No matter how much explanations we are given, if God does not grant us access, we will never understand. When we understand divine things, it is because God has granted us access to His secrets.

> *When pride comes, then comes shame; but with the humble is wisdom. (Proverbs 11:2)*

The position of humility is maintaining a teachable disposition. Boldly make this declaration, "**I have a teachable spirit.**

**I am not above correction. God can choose to teach me through anyone, and at any time, Amen.**" So shall it be in Jesus' mighty name.

> *Good and upright is the Lord; therefore He teaches sinners in the way. The humble He guides in justice, and the humble He teaches His way. (Psalms 25:8-9)*

The best teacher is the Holy Spirit. When we humble ourselves to learn from anyone that is under God's authority, we open ourselves to the teaching ministry of the Holy Spirit. The Holy Spirit can use analogies to help you understand what is being taught. He can even correct the things (e.g. mistakes and errors) we are being taught.

## An Insatiable Thirst for Knowledge

A thirst is what it takes to keep receiving until your cup of knowledge and understanding runs over.

> *Ho! Everyone who thirsts, come to the waters; And you who have no money, come, buy and eat. Yes, come, buy wine and milk without money and without price. Why do you spend money for what is not bread, and your wages for what does not satisfy? Listen carefully to Me, and eat what is good, and let your soul delight itself in abundance. Incline your ear, and come to Me. Hear, and your soul shall live; And I will make an everlasting covenant with you— The sure mercies of David. (Isaiah 55:1-3)*

God only satisfies those that are genuinely thirsty. From Isaiah 55:1-3, you can see the value placed on a genuine thirst. When there is a thirst, there will always be a way. The story is told of Michael Faraday, who as a teenager skipped meals regularly just to buy books to read.

Why should we have an insatiable thirst for knowledge? There is always more to learn, and no one can ever know everything, except God. There are some other reasons to have an insatiable desire for knowledge.

## There is Always More to Learn

No matter how much you know, there is always more to know. Knowledge is highly elastic. It is unending.

> *And if anyone thinks that he knows anything, he knows nothing yet as he ought to know. (1 Corinthians 8:2)*

This simply means that we need to cultivate the understanding that there is always more to add, to what we already know. This was true in the case of Apollos (Acts 18:24-28). He already knew a lot, but there was more he could know. When he submitted himself to more learning, his effectiveness and efficiency multiplied.

## Rejection or Destruction

Lack of knowledge is not only when we don't have knowledge, but also when we don't have enough knowledge. Lack of knowledge can lead a believer to destruction. It can also cause God to reject a believer.

*My people are destroyed for lack of knowledge. Because you have rejected knowledge, I also will reject you from being priest for Me; because you have forgotten the law of your God, I also will forget your children. (Hosea 4:6)*

### Knowledge leads to increase

One of the key ingredients of success is knowledge. In fact, an increase in knowledge always leads to an increase in success. This is why it is said that "leaders are readers." An increase in knowledge expands our horizon, which can lead to greater attainment.

*that I may know Him and the power of His resurrection, and the fellowship of His sufferings, being conformed to His death, if, by any means, I may attain to the resurrection from the dead. Not that I have already attained, or am already perfected; but I press on, that I may lay hold of that for which Christ Jesus has also laid hold of me. Brethren, I do not count myself to have apprehended; but one thing I do, forgetting those things which are behind and reaching forward to those things which are ahead, I press toward the goal for the prize of the upward call of God in Christ Jesus. Therefore let us, as many as are mature, have this mind; and if in anything you think otherwise, God will reveal even this to you. (Philippians 3:10-15)*

Paul started by expressing his strong desire to know God more. Subsequently, we see that as he began to know God more, he was more empowered to press towards the goal for the prize of the upward call of God in Christ Jesus. This kind of thinking (or mindset) is for those that are mature. It takes maturity to put aside what you already know and what you have already achieved, just to gain more knowledge.

May God help you to consistently have a thirst to know more of the right things in Jesus' name.

## Eliminate Distraction

A disciplined mind must be one that is free from distractions. The world we live in today is full of different kinds of distractions. Some are external, while the most lethal ones are internal. We must discipline ourselves not to allow distractions whenever we are about to learn. It is important that this becomes a habit, because learning can be planned or unplanned. As technology also becomes more prevalent, we must ensure that we are avoiding distractions.

> *[looking away from all that will distract us and] focusing our eyes on Jesus*, who is the Author and Perfecter of faith [the first incentive for our belief and the One who brings our faith to maturity], who for the joy [of accomplishing the goal] set before Him endured the cross, disregarding the shame, and sat down at the right hand of the throne of God [revealing His deity, His authority, and the completion of His work]. (Hebrews 12:2 AMP)

We see in Hebrews 12:2 that in order to learn from Jesus, we need to look away from all that will distract us, and focus our eyes on Jesus. This looking away from all that will distract us is not just our physical eyes alone, it also includes our thoughts and emotions.

We can achieve this by always being in the moment. The Bible even urges us to guard up the loins of our minds (1 Peter 1:13). This means that we can control our thoughts and our physical eyes. When you are settling down to learn, consciously block out every conflicting internal conversation. Avoid the trap of multitasking when learning. If you are learning and browsing through social media at the same time, you will not fully assimilate what you're learning.

It is not just enough to avoid distractions, you also need to consciously focus your attention on the person you are learning from. Since the Holy Spirit is also our teacher (John 14:26), we ought to focus our attention on Him especially during those teaching moments.

**Focus**

A wise person once said, "If you chase two rabbits, both will escape."

I define focus as operating with singleness of mind in order to achieve a set goal. The Bible advises us thus, "*Let your eyes look straight ahead, and your eyelids look right before you*" (Proverbs 4:25).

When you are driving at a low speed, you can afford to look around and notice everything happening around you. Perhaps you would have noticed that when driving at higher speeds, you cannot afford to lose your focus on the road. A split-second distraction can be deadly. To remain a success, your height (altitude) in life must be directly proportional to your focus; the higher you go, the more the focus you require to thrive and go higher. This is the reason why a high-performing CEO only focuses their attention on a few key metrics. The high-performing CEO cannot afford to monitor every single metric. There are many things clamoring for their attention at that level, and they cannot afford to lose focus.

Focus involves both self-discipline, and the wisdom to choose. It is very possible to misconstrue focus to mean; only applying self-discipline in order to pay attention to something. This, however, is an incomplete picture. If you fix your attention on the wrong things, though you are applying self-discipline, you are still acting without wisdom. We find an example of this in the story of Mary and Martha.

> *Now it happened as they went that He entered a certain village; and a certain woman named Martha welcomed Him into her house. And she had a sister called Mary, who also sat at Jesus' feet and heard His word. But Martha was distracted with much serving, and she approached Him and said, "Lord, do You not care that my sister has left me to serve alone? Therefore tell her to help me." And Jesus answered and said to her, "Martha, Martha, you are worried and troubled about many things. But one thing is needed, and Mary has chosen that good part, which will not be taken away from her." (Luke 10:38-42)*

In this story, we see that Mary demonstrated both wisdom and self-discipline by choosing the right activity; she focused her attention on Jesus' teachings. Martha, on the other hand, demonstrated only self-discipline; she focused her attention on serving Jesus and his disciples, instead of Jesus' teachings. There are many who diligently focus on enjoying sports at the expense of other vital activities. They can focus on playing video games, instead of picking up their kids from school. They know all the players' statistics offhand, yet they do not remember their spouse's birthday, or their anniversary. This is a high-level display of folly.

The Bible tells us that we have the ability to choose life or death (Deuteronomy 30:19).

The first step in focus is to exercise your ability to choose by asking yourself "what is the wisest thing to do now?" Breakdown your day into segments, and predetermine the best thing to do during each of those segments. Without predetermination, i.e. having a schedule, it will be very easy for anything and everything that looks good to grab our attention.

After choosing the activity to engage in, joyfully engage in it with all your heart.

> *Whatever you do [whatever your task may be], work from the soul [that is, put in your very best effort], as [something done] for the Lord and not for men. (Colossians 3:23 AMP)*

Don't be one of those that are in one place, but their hearts are somewhere else. Have you ever engaged in a conversation with someone where they told you their name, but you did not remember afterwards? Are you one of those that go to church, but their minds are thinking about what they could have been doing at home? Resist that double-mindedness at once. It can make you unstable in all your ways (James 1:8).

Maintaining focus while learning helps your mind to receive information. You cannot process information that you cannot remember. So far, we have explored the kind of information to be received, how to position ourselves to receive this information, and the need to be focused. Once we have now done all these, the next question is how to process this information. This leads us to the next major point, which is processing information.

**Processing Information**

It is good to have information, but not profiting from it is a sad state to be in. You often find very knowledgeable people using information to gloat and be condescending to others. This is because they do not know how to profit from the information they have accumulated.

Remember, I mentioned earlier that understanding is a gift from God. He is the one that allows us access to knowledge (or revelation) that we can profit with. From the parable of talents (Matthew 25:14-30), we understand that we will give account of the gifts (tangible or intangible) that we have been given by God.

The Bible even goes a step further by calling a person that does not roast his prey a lazy person.

> *The lazy man does not roast what he took in hunting, but diligence is man's precious possession. (Proverbs 12:27)*

We actively or passively hunt for information. The brain is the processor of information that was received in different formats. What we do with this information will determine if we are lazy or diligent.

This passage goes further to explain the danger of laziness with regards to processing information.

> *I went by the field of the lazy man, and by the vineyard of the man devoid of understanding; and there it was, all overgrown with thorns; Its surface was covered with nettles; Its stone wall was broken down. When I saw it, I considered it well; I looked on it and received instruction: a little sleep, a little slumber, a little folding of the hands to rest; so shall your poverty come like a prowler, and your need like an armed man. (Proverbs 24:30-34)*

The field or vineyard of the lazy man can be likened to his mind. Our minds can be overgrown with thorns and nettles. The walls can even be broken down, if we do not tend to our garden. The writer of proverbs diagnosed the problem to be as a result of laziness, not necessarily the devil. It is sad that many Christians are quick to attribute every single misfortune to the devil. By simply being lazy mentally, you are already causing destruction to your own mind.

## The Power of Asking Questions

In order to receive information, you need to properly position yourself. In order to process information, you need to ask the right questions. If you are not asking questions, you are not processing information. Questions are the sickle with which we harvest valuables from the information we gather. The questions can be internally (asking yourself) or externally (asking the one sharing the information).

The mind of Jesus is the best mind there ever was and will ever be. He displayed excellence while on the earth. He responded to the Pharisees and Sadducees in ways that left them speechless. His actions are still being studied in churches, schools, boardrooms, and many other places, till today. A passage in the Bible gives us an insight into how Jesus processed information.

> *His parents went to Jerusalem every year at the Feast of the Passover. And when He was twelve years old, they went up to Jerusalem according to the custom of the feast. When they had finished the days, as they returned, the Boy Jesus lingered behind in Jerusalem. And Joseph and His mother did not know it; but supposing Him to have been in the company, they went a day's journey, and sought Him among their relatives and acquaintances. So when they did not find Him, they returned to Jerusalem, seeking Him.* **Now so it was that after three days they found Him in the temple, sitting in the midst of the teachers, both listening to them**

*and asking them questions.* *And all who heard Him were astonished at His understanding and an-* *swers. (Luke 2:41-47)*

Jesus was listening to the teachers (he positioned Himself to learn - humility, focus, etc.) and asking questions (processing what He was hearing). Do you want to be like Jesus? Ask the questions. If you are afraid of asking questions, it shows that you have some character flaws to resolve. It could be a sign of low self-esteem, fear, pride, etc.

> **I decree in the mighty name of Jesus, everything stopping you from asking the right questions, be destroyed now!**

As a teacher, one major way I know my students are paying attention and learning, is by the questions they ask. Here are some questions you can ask, to enable you to learn better.

## 6 Critical Thinking Questions

The specific kinds of question to ask is dependent on the material. There are, however, guides to help us ask questions that will enable us to properly process the information we are receiving. They are called the 5Ws and 1H. It involves asking who, what, when, why, where and how. You will hardly have the opportunity to ask all these questions at the same time.

For example, if you are receiving information about a new business opportunity, you can utilize these six critical thinking questions in helping you process the information you are receiving.

**You can ask "who" related questions like:**

> Who are those involved in this business venture?
> Who has successfully profited from this business?
> Who are my customers?
> Who are my suppliers or vendors?

**You can ask "what" related questions like:**

> What is this business about?
> What kind of product or service will be provided to customers?
> What is the profit margin?
> What kind of expenses will be incurred?

**You can ask "when" related questions like:**

> When should I expect to break-even?
> When can I come onboard?

**You can ask "where" related questions like:**

> Where did this business originate from?
> Where is this business currently thriving the most?
> Where else do you think this business will thrive?

**You can ask "why" related questions like:**

> Why are you sharing this information with me?
> Why is this a viable business opportunity?
> Why should I get involved in this business?

**You can ask "how" related questions like:**

> How much capital do I need to get started?
> How can I make the products?
> How should I differentiate myself from others?
> How can I profit from this information?

You can see that if you can ask the right questions to the right person, your chances of getting the right answers are much higher.

If this was likened to eating, this would be the chewing stage. While eating, your entire mouth is put to work. Sometimes, even your head feels the effect of chewing. At the end of the day, you know that your body is getting the nutrients it needs to survive.

It takes effort to process information. This is probably why most people run away from it. This is where real value lies. If you can discipline yourself to properly listen and ask the right questions, your mind will produce great outputs. Receive grace to put in the effort to process the information that God richly makes available to you in Jesus' name.

**Storing Information**

You can receive and process information properly, but may not store that information properly. As a Pastor, I have noticed that a large number of people claim to suffer from memory loss. Many people claim an inability to remember people's names, faces, etc. Even though some of those claims are legitimate, most of them are not. I used to be among those that claimed an inability to remember people's names, faces, or other important details, until I found the way out. Praise God!

At a very high level, a human being's memory is divided into short term and long term. The short-term memory stores information that is gathered every second, minute, day, and week. The long-term memory, on the other hand, stores information that can be retrieved after a few weeks, months, and even years. Information flows from the short-term memory to the long-term memory. Many times, when people complain about their inability to remember details, they are simply saying that they are unable to successfully move information from their short-term memory to their long-term memory.

A person can successfully apply the principles discussed so far, but still be unable to store information for future retrieval.

While short term memory can be affected by lack of focus, attention, interest, and other things, long term memory can be affected by an inability to keep records. Using computer parlance, the RAM (Random Access Memory) is the short-term memory. while the hard drive is the long-term memory. Please note that this does not include other events like accidents, illnesses, and suchlike that can also affect a person's memory. Those are exceptions and will not be referenced while discussing this topic.

The short-term memory is designed to remember the information being processed by the mind. The moment the processing stage is over, the information is expected to be stored away or else the mind will delete the information, regardless of how valuable it is.

If you follow the guidelines stated earlier about processing information, you will have a very sound short-term memory. If you follow the guidelines stated in this chapter, you will have a sound long term memory.

### Document critical information

God keeps records of key information. These Bible verses make it clear that God keeps long term records of information. If God does it, we ought to do the same.

*And anyone not found written in the* **Book of Life** *was cast into the lake of fire. (Revelation 20:15)*

*And I urge you also, true companion, help these women who labored with me in the gospel, with Clement also, and the rest of my fellow workers, whose names are in the* **Book of Life.** *(Philippians 4:3)*

*He who overcomes shall be clothed in white garments, and I will not blot out his name from the* **Book of Life;** *but I will confess his name before My Father and before His angels. (Revelations 3:5)*

*Your eyes saw my substance, being yet unformed. And in* **Your book** *they all were written, the days fashioned for me, when as yet there were none of them. (Psalms 139:16)*

To have a sound long term memory, discipline yourself by having a journal where you store critical information. This journal (personal book of life) can be hard copy or electronic. I am in favor of electronic records, because they are searchable, can be password-protected, portable, and easily preserved.

I have explored several notes, or journaling applications, and have settled with the Daily Notes application on the iPad or iPhone. You can conduct a search online for one that meets your needs.

When you encounter key information, immediately document its details in your journal. Enter enough information in the journal to help you remember the event many years later. Please remember the characteristics of good information that we discussed earlier. I do not advise documenting information that does not meet the criteria in Philippians 4:8. This practice is better suited for recording testimonies you never want to forget.

Examples of details to be stored are linked to the six critical thinking questions we discussed earlier. You can even add pictures to your records, to aid recollection.

> What happened?
> When did it happen?
> With whom did it happen?
> How did it happen?
> Where did it happen?
> How did you feel when it happened?
> Why do you think it happened?
> Any other incidental information?

A good record will facilitate your reenactment of events that occurred. It will enable you to effortlessly recollect information. This simple habit will enhance your long-term memory. In no time, many will refer to you as a person with an excellent memory.

P.S. Don't forget to recommend this book to them.

Do you want your story to be told properly? If yes, begin right now to document your own story.

### Regularly Review Critical Information

The story is told of King Xerxes who, on a particular day, could not sleep, and requested that the book of the records of the chronicles be read out to him. In Esther 6:1-3, the scripture said:

> *That night the king could not sleep. So one was commanded to bring the book of the records of the chronicles; and they were read before the king. And it was found written that Mordecai had told of Bigthana and Teresh, two of the king's eunuchs, the doorkeepers who had sought to lay hands on King Ahasuerus. Then the king said, "What honor or dignity has been bestowed on Mordecai for this?" And the king's servants who attended him said, "Nothing has been done for him."*

This story shows that it was a common practice for Kings to review documented records. The more you review your documented records, the quicker you will be able to recollect them.

Have you ever found yourself in a situation where you were unable to remember a significant testimony that happened in your life? The practice of documenting and reviewing key information will help keep that information at your finger-tips.

You can determine to review your key documented records on a weekly basis. Perhaps on Saturday mornings or Sunday evenings, before another working week begins. You could also determine to review it on a monthly basis. This will also enhance your faith and gratitude.

In Deuteronomy 8, God strongly warned the children of Israel not to forget Him, and all that He had done for them. Applying the recommendation from this book will help you and I remember noteworthy events in our lives.

As you practice the recommendations from this chapter, I foresee you enjoying benefits like better communication, because *"out of the abundance of the heart, the mouth speaks"* (Luke 6:45). It will also be more difficult for evil communication to proceed from your mouth (Ephesians 4:29).

# 5

## DISCIPLINED HABITS

A habit is something a person does naturally, without thinking.

Habits can be a powerful force, or a destructive one. They can either make, or break a person. Habits are powered by the human will. Using our ability to choose, we can change habits and develop new ones.

Many people struggle with changing bad habits and developing good ones. Below is an analogy that will help you understand the way habits are formed.

### Forming New Habits

The way habits are formed is similar to the way a plane takes off to its destination. They are divided into five stages. Initial excitement, reduced excitement, self-doubt, normalization, and regained excitement.

### Initial Excitement Stage

At the beginning point of a new habit, there has to be enough excitement in order for the habit to take off. Like a plane, it cannot simply take off the way a helicopter takes off. It has to accelerate on the runway to generate enough speed. We must build up the excitement for the new habit. This can be done by joining a support group, gathering inspirational materials that promotes the benefits of acquiring this habit. All these should happen before you begin forming the habit.

### Reduced Excitement Stage

When the initial excitement has been gathered and you have started with the habit, you might never be able to see yourself quitting the habit. Research shows that most people quit their gym membership after the first few weeks in January. This is because of the reduced excitement stage.

This stage is similar to what the plane experiences after it has taken off. After takeoff, it seems like the plane is not moving fast anymore. Remember that the perception of speed on the ground is different from the perception of speed in the air. We all know that even though it does not feel like the plane is moving, immediately after takeoff, it is indeed moving.

When you reach this phase while forming a new habit, relax, you are still moving forward. You must simply make sure that you are continuing with the habit, even though you don't feel as excited as you felt in the beginning.

This stage emphasizes the perceived loss of the emotions of excitement, joy, etc. As mentioned earlier in this chapter, the will is very important in adopting and maintaining habits.

When the emotions are struggling, the will is what keeps you going, especially in this stage. If you feel like you naturally have a weak will, being accountable to someone you respect can keep you from giving up.

## Self-Doubt Stage

In this stage, the reduced excited can now begin to affect your thinking. This is the most difficult stage in forming a new habit. Most people fall off either in the reduced excitement stage, or in this self-doubt stage.

The plane has taken off, and is now trying to break through the clouds in order to maintain a cruising altitude. During this time, the seat belt sign is still on, because it is not yet safe to walk around. There is still a risk of turbulence. There is still a risk that the plane might go down.

In this stage, people begin to doubt their decision to form the new habit. They begin to challenge the assumptions that they had before forming the habit. They also begin struggling with thoughts of quitting.

The reduced excitement stage focuses a lot more on the emotions while this self-doubt stage focuses on the mind. A strong will is what will keep you going at this stage. It can last for a short time or a long time, but one thing I know for sure is that if you endure till the end, you will reap the fruit from the new habit.

This is not the stage to become relaxed. Just like the example of the plane, this is not the time to remove your seat belt and feel comfortable in the plane. This is not the stage to sleep through your alarm. This is not the time to entertain the idea of cheat days from exercise or eating healthy. This is why cheat days for some people might become cheat weeks, and then cheat years.

## Normalization Stage

The next stage is normalization. At this stage, the new habit has formed. You are no longer thinking about it too much before engaging in the habit. You simply think about the activity once, and decide to do it. The excitement has not yet returned, but you are not bothered. You have learned to press ahead with the activity, regardless of the fact that you are not excited.

In the example of a plane, this is when the plane has reached cruising altitude. At this point, the seat belt sign is removed, and people can move freely in the plane. Even meals can be served on the plane at this point.

In the normalization stage, you can afford to take one cheat day without feeling the need to extend it to two or more cheat days. If it's a habit to read your Bible regularly, and you have been doing it in the mornings, you can be able to move it to the afternoon or evening without breaking the habit. It has now become part of you. This is a good stage to be in, but it is not the ultimate goal. Using the plane example, even during this normalization stage, there could still be turbulence in the air, if the plane encounters thick clouds. Even though the chances are slimmer, a habit can still be lost at this stage. It might be difficult, but given the right circumstances, intensity and frequency, the newly formed habit can still be jettisoned.

## Regained Excitement Stage

This is the ideal stage to get to for every habit. This is the stage where the will is strong, excitement has been regained, and the mind sees more reasons to remain committed to the habit.

At this stage, even if you are paid to abandon the habit you will most likely not accept the payment. At this stage, you are now living the dream. You are an inspiration to other people that want to adopt the same habit. You are now a role model. You are able to respond to questions about your habit in glowing terms. This is the stage where you can declare like Paul, *"who shall separate us from the love of Christ..."*

> *Who shall separate us from the love of Christ? Shall tribulation, or distress, or persecution, or famine, or nakedness, or peril, or sword? As it is written: "for Your sake we are killed all day long; we are accounted as sheep for the slaughter." Yet in all these things we are more than conquerors through Him who loved us. For I am persuaded that neither death nor life, nor angels nor principalities nor powers, nor things present nor things to come, nor height nor depth, nor any other created thing, shall be able to separate us from the love of God which is in Christ Jesus our Lord. (Romans 8:35-39)*

As you develop a new habit, keep these stages in mind, and let them encourage you. If you find yourself in the other stages, you know that you just need to keep engaging in the habit. Eventually, you will get to the regained excitement stage, where the habit has formed, and you're excited about it.

## A Disciplined Will

The human will is what allows us to make decisions and stick to them. It is that part of us that enables us to say, "See you at 9:00 a.m.," and actually be there at 9:00 a.m. as promised. Remember, God made man in His own image (Genesis 1:26). Therefore, God Himself has a will. Jesus taught us to pray for God's will to be done on earth as it is in heaven.

> *Your kingdom come. Your will be done on earth as it is in heaven. (Matthew 6:10)*

Jesus also prayed for God's will to be done concerning the nature of His death.

> *Saying, "Father, if it is Your will, take this cup away from Me; nevertheless not My will, but Yours, be done." (Luke 22:42)*

People often wrongfully castigate those that have strong will as being stubborn. This sometimes causes them to resent this God-given strength. A strong will is not a liability, it is a vital asset that guarantees success in life. It only becomes a liability if unused or used without wisdom.

A disciplined will is one that is able to say "no" and mean "no". A disciplined will is one that is able to say "yes" and mean "yes".

An undisciplined will is what makes people succumb to peer pressure. Make no mistake, peer pressure is not limited to kids alone. It also affects adults. Peer pressure in adults is what makes them buy things they cannot afford, in order to fit in. It is what makes an adult compromise on their faith among work colleagues or friends. It is what makes people of all ages unable to make a decision.

Jesus had a disciplined will. He was able to make decisions and stick to them. He was able to take a stand and maintain that stand, regardless of the opposition; even when it led to death.

A person with a disciplined will puts principles above pleasure. They put following their conscience above convenience. This kind of discipline is what makes a believer decide they will not sin against God.

The human will is primarily disciplined using the Word of God. You feed the strength of your will based on the written or revealed Word of God. Every time you encounter a Word of God and agree to follow whatever it asks you to do, your will is empowered. In essence, you gain more willpower.

## Characteristics of a Disciplined Will

### Determination
One of the outputs of a disciplined will is determination. Determination simply refers to the ability to keep going and not give up until victory is secured. The Bible paints the following pictures of determination.

> Look, a people rises like a lioness, and lifts itself up like a lion; It shall not lie down until it devours the prey, and drinks the blood of the slain. (Numbers 23:24)

> *For the Lord God will help me; therefore I will not be*
> *disgraced; therefore I have set my face like a flint, and I*
> *know that I will not be ashamed. (Isaiah 50:7)*
> *For I determined not to know anything among you except*
> *Jesus Christ and Him crucified. (1 Corinthians 2:2)*

Is it possible to succeed without determination? Absolutely not. A successful person is able to keep going even when odds are against them. They are able to keep going even when people are against them.

A stubborn person, and a determined person both have a disciplined will. The difference between them is that a stubborn person will keep going, even though they are going in the wrong direction, while a determined person will keep going in the right direction, no matter the internal or external opposition. Stubbornness is destructive, but determination is very profitable.

Determination will enable you to finish things you start. A determined person does not allow their emotions to hinder them from doing what needs to be done.

Do you give up easily? Do you change your mind easily? Do you back down when threatened? These are all signs of insufficient or lack of determination.

One of David's men distinguished himself by the determination he displayed. He dug in, and fought until he won the battle.

> *And after him was Shammah the son of Agee the*
> *Hararite. The Philistines had gathered together into a*

*troop where there was a piece of ground full of lentils.*
*So the people fled from the Philistines. But he stationed*
*himself in the middle of the field, defended it, and killed*
*the Philistines. So the Lord brought about a great vic-*
*tory. (2 Samuel 23:11-12)*

Another story is told of Esther's decision to risk her life by vio-
lating King Xerxes' policy. She made up her mind that regardless of what happened, because her people were in danger, she
will appear before the King. She made a statement that oozes
with determination and boldness. She said, *"if I perish, I perish."*

*Go, gather together all the Jews that are present in*
*Shushan, and fast ye for me, and neither eat nor drink*
*three days, night or day: I also and my maidens will*
*fast likewise; and so will I go in unto the king, which*
*is not according to the law: and if I perish, I perish.*
*(Esther 4:16)*

Determination, otherwise known as a disciplined will, is so
crucial because there are always obstacles in the path of everyone that does great things.

I remember when God called me into ministry to start
Cornerstone Christian Church of God. I experienced lots of
disappointments and setbacks. Where I was expecting encour-
agement, I experienced discouragement. At a point, I was even
mulling over the idea of disobeying God amidst the doubt of
God's calling over my life. One day as I was driving home after
church and thinking about the call of God on my life, I uttered

the words that Esther is famous for. I said, "I cannot claim not to have heard God. I will proceed with His assignment; if I perish I perish." That was when determination was infused in me for the assignment God has given me.

Declare this with me, "**If I perish I perish. I must do what God has called me to do, in Jesus' name**".

## Delayed Gratification

Delayed gratification is our ability to work now in order to play later. This inability has shipwrecked many glorious destinies. It takes a strong will to defer certain pleasures until a later date.

The inability to delay gratification till the appropriate time has caused many to engage in premarital sex. It has caused many to hastily marry the wrong person. It has caused many to put off savings and investment, in order to have fun. It has caused many to spend the money they ought to give to God as tithes, offerings or special seeds.

In fact, the temptations Jesus experienced were overcome also, because He had a strong will to delay gratification. The things the devil offered him in the first two temptations were going to be His, after a while. After His fast, He was going to be able to eat bread. After resurrection, He was going to be given authority over all again.

> *Looking unto Jesus, the author and finisher of our faith, who for the joy that was set before Him endured the cross, despising the shame, and has sat down at the right hand of the throne of God. (Hebrews 12:2)*

> *Therefore I also, after I heard of your faith in the Lord
> Jesus and your love for all the saints, do not cease to
> give thanks for you, making mention of you in my
> prayers: that the God of our Lord Jesus Christ, the
> Father of glory, may give to you the spirit of wisdom
> and revelation in the knowledge of Him, the eyes of
> your understanding being enlightened; that you may
> know what is the hope of His calling, what are the
> riches of the glory of His inheritance in the saints, and
> what is the exceeding greatness of His power toward
> us who believe, according to the working of His mighty
> power which He worked in Christ when He raised
> Him from the dead and seated Him at His right hand
> in the heavenly places, far above all principality and
> power and might and dominion, and every name that
> is named, not only in this age but also in that which
> is to come. And He put all things under His feet, and
> gave Him to be head over all things to the church, 23
> which is His body, the fullness of Him who fills all in
> all. (Ephesians 1:15-23)*

Delayed gratification can be exercised using a strong will.
Wisdom enables us to make the right decisions, while a strong
will enables us to stick to the decisions we made, as long as
they are still valid. It will enable you to fast when you have to.
It will enable you to spend time with God, instead of the many
distractions clamoring for your time. It will enable you delay
celebration until the victory is permanently won. David did

not celebrate his defeat over Goliath until he cut off Goliath's head (1 Samuel 17:48-51). The ability to delay gratification will enable you to apply self-control when needed.

Even though the Bible classifies self-control as one of the fruit of the Holy Spirit, self-control is displayed by the will. The stronger your self-control, the stronger your ability to delay gratification.

## Excellence

There is nothing excellent on its own. It is a human's extraordinary input that makes something excellent. A strong will enables a person to consistently pay the price to be excellent. A strong will is needed because many people will kick against it and you need to be able to stand your ground.

Excellence is achieved by the application of wisdom, but also an ability to consistently pay the price of sacrifice. A strong will is going to enable you to stay on a task or an activity until the desired excellent result is achieved. Long after others have given up, a person with a strong will is still going, till the excellent result is attained.

There is a reason we are able to pay more for excellent products. They have sown the seed of excellence, and we are bound to pay them for that extraordinary effort.

Excellence will make you accept only the best work from yourself. You internally drive yourself to deliver excellence all the time.

Excellence requires an input of more time and effort. Perhaps that is why many cannot pay the price to attain it.

It is a very costly virtue, but it carries lots of benefits. The Bible had a lot to say about the excellence that Daniel diligently displayed.

> *Inasmuch as an excellent spirit, knowledge, understanding, interpreting dreams, solving riddles, and explaining enigmas were found in this Daniel, whom the king named Belteshazzar, now let Daniel be called, and he will give the interpretation." (Daniel 5:12)*
> *Then this Daniel distinguished himself above the governors and satraps, because an excellent spirit was in him; and the king gave thought to setting him over the whole realm. (Daniel 6:3)*

The Word of God tells us that if we ask, we will receive (Matthew 7:7). I pray in the mighty name of Jesus Christ that an excellent spirit is coming upon you now!

### Time Management

The ability to keep to time is a function of discipline. Consistently honoring time commitments is a display of discipline.

Discipline enhances the value of our lives. Time is not only in years. It's also in months, weeks, days, hours, minutes and seconds. Discipline in time management is making the best of each moment of time.

How productively we engage the moments of the day determines the outcome of our lives. Make the most of every amount of time that you have.

Time management goes beyond showing up on time, or concluding a speaking engagement on time. It extends to a person's holistic use of time. It extends to keeping a schedule, planning the tasks for the day.

A lot has been written about tools that can be used to manage time and enhance one's productivity. This section will be mainly focused on the bigger picture that makes the other daily time management techniques effective.

I will be discussing the cycle principle. It is something that the Holy Spirit taught me in 2017. I had been practicing bits and pieces of it before then, but He gave me a more holistic view of this principle.

## The Cycle Principle

Everything that God created follows a cycle. We sometimes call those cycles, seasons. Every cycle is measured in units of time. Every cycle that God created is designed to have definite fruits at the end, or else it results in a waste.

Take a woman's menstrual cycle as an example. On average the cycle lasts for 28 days. During the cycle, the ovaries produce eggs for fertilization. When those eggs are not fertilized after the cycle, as if in disappointment, the uterus sheds its linings and it results in a menstrual flow.

When God was creating the heavens and the earth in Genesis 1, we are told that every morning and evening during the six days produced definite results. In that example, the cycles were morning and evening. Each cycle ended with God looking at His output and saying it was very good.

Effective time management involves dividing your time in cycles and having defined outputs from each cycle. Depending on your tasks, it could be cycles of minutes, hours, days, months, quarters, years, etc.

> *So teach us to number our days that we may gain a heart of wisdom. (Psalms 90:12)*

It takes wisdom to know how to divide our days on earth, i.e. to number our days. The Bible even recommends that more difficult tasks should be done during one's youth (Lamentations 3:27).

From where you are, begin by locating God's plan for your life. Where do you see yourself ending up according to God's plan? This is the destination. With that destination in mind, you can now begin to draw out the cycles based on how far you can see.

> *For which of you, intending to build a tower, does not sit down first and count the cost, whether he has enough to finish it. (Luke 14:28)*

Your life is the tower, and you need to sit down to count the cost for the end result that you have seen in mind.

Determine the stages of the "tower" that you can see: your youth, young adult, adult, and senior days. Life is in stages, and those that prepare adequately for each stage are those that succeed. If you are a youth now and are eating uncontrollably and not exercising, all things being equal, at least your adult stage and beyond will be riddled with health challenges.

Your plan does not have to be perfect, but you will be planning to fail if you fail to plan. There is a popular saying that goes thus "*man proposes but God disposes.*" It is based on Proverbs 19:21, "*there are many plans in a man's heart, nevertheless the Lord's counsel—that will stand.*" TLB's rendering of Proverbs 19:21 is "*man proposes, but God disposes*". This does not mean that man ought not to make plans. We are expected to make plans with our minds and in conjunction with the Holy Spirit.

Once the stages (every twenty years) have been determined, you can then begin to plan your next ten-year blocks, then five-year blocks, etc. All these have to happen before you can then begin to plan for the year, each quarter, months, weeks, days and hours. For this to be effective, each of these cycles must have definite outputs, or expected results.

Of all the concepts shared in this book, this might be the most challenging, but also one of the most rewarding. By simply setting clear goals for each of these cycles, you are already setting yourself up to succeed.

The devil's mission statement is very clear. It is to steal, kill and destroy (John 10:10). If the devil can succeed in distracting you from getting results from your cycles, he has succeeded in stealing your time. If the devil can successfully steal your time, he has succeeded in stealing from you, killing you, and eventually destroying your destiny. Make up your mind now, to never allow that to happen.

Here is an example of cycles and goals using the stages of a person's life:

> **Youth Cycle** – determine my purpose and what it takes to achieve it
>
> **Young Adult Cycle** – finalize all foundation elements for achieving my purpose, e.g. Master's degree, certification courses, etc. Identify the pacesetters in that field and understudy them.
>
> **Adult Cycle** – fully commit myself to my purpose
>
> **Senior Cycle** – fully commit myself to training others to be better than me. Prepare to see Jesus.

Bishop David Oyedepo is quoted as saying, *"life is in stages and men are in sizes."* When you have an idea of the steps to get to your goal and you are taking those steps, it will be easier to be confident about the future.

Right away, block off some time to count the costs for the tower you intend to build. Right away, block off some time to determine where you intend to be during the different stages in your life. Then, and only then, will your daily discipline yield results.

I pray that God will give you the grace to pay the price in implementing the cycle principle in your life and in all your endeavors.

# 6

# A DISCIPLINED SPIRIT

The human spirit is different from the Holy Spirit. The Holy Spirit is the Spirit from God that we are given access to when we become born again. The part of man that connects with the Holy Spirit at redemption is the human spirit. When we say that we are filled with the Holy Spirit, what we are saying in essence is that we have given the Holy Spirit free access to our human spirit.

Let's see what the Bible says about the distinction between the Holy Spirit, and the human spirit.

> *For what man knows the things of a man except the spirit of the man which is in him? Even so no one knows the things of God except the Spirit of God. (1 Corinthians 2:11)*

This passage clearly shows that there is a distinction between the Holy Spirit, and the human spirit. The real human being is his spirit. The human spirit is the most intimate part of man. According to 1 Corinthians 2:11, nothing is hidden from the spirit of a man.

In Romans 8:16, the Bible again clearly distinguishes between the human spirit and the Holy Spirit.

> *The Spirit Himself bears witness with our spirit that we*
> *are children of God. (Romans 8:16)*

The Spirit referenced in capital letters is the Holy Spirit. This is the Spirit of God that we are given access to at redemption. When we receive the Pentecostal experience of an infilling of the Holy Spirit, or the baptism of the Holy Spirit, it is simply a more intense experience where we allow the Holy Spirit to have a deeper access into our being.

What then is a disciplined human spirit? A disciplined human spirit is one that only accepts and follows instructions that came directly and indirectly from the Holy Spirit and/or the word of God.

Jesus had a disciplined spirit when He was on the earth. These were words that proceeded from Jesus Himself that attests to this.

> *Then Jesus answered and said to them, most assuredly,*
> *I say to you, the Son can do nothing of Himself, but*
> *what He sees the Father do; for whatever He does, the*

> *Son also does in like manner. For the Father loves the Son, and shows Him all things that He Himself does; and He will show Him greater works than these, that you may marvel. For as the Father raises the dead and gives life to them, even so the Son gives life to whom He will. (John 5:19-21)*
>
> *I can of Myself do nothing. As I hear, I judge; and My judgment is righteous, because I do not seek My own will but the will of the Father who sent Me. (John 5:30)*

Do you see that Jesus had a disciplined Spirit? His Spirit, while on the earth, only received and accepted instructions from the written word, and the Holy Spirit. In the beginning of His ministry, the Bible tells us that Jesus was led by the Holy Spirit into the wilderness where He was tempted by the devil. Jesus had discernment, therefore He must have known what would happen in the wilderness. He still succumbed to the leading of the Holy Spirit.

> *Then Jesus, being filled with the Holy Spirit, returned from the Jordan and was led by the Spirit into the wilderness, being tempted for forty days by the devil. And in those days He ate nothing, and afterward, when they had ended, He was hungry. (Luke 4:1-2)*

Jesus was able to turn the stone into bread as instructed by the devil. He was also able to throw Himself down from the top of the temple as instructed by the devil. In those two temptations, the issue wasn't that Jesus could not do it. The issue was that He does not receive instructions from the devil. This is the mark of a disciplined spirit.

A disciplined spirit is able to properly differentiate the things of God from that of the devil, and is determined to only submit to the will of God.

An undisciplined spirit consumes materials from both God and the devil. An undisciplined spirit does not carefully ensure that they are only obeying God. It follows the loudest voice.

### How to Discipline the Human Spirit

God is no respecter of persons (Acts 10:34). If there are any spiritual giants, it simply means that they follow a consistent, biblically acceptable, spiritual regimen. This is what gives them the command of spiritual things.

There are ways we can discipline the human spirit. The same way the human body and soul can be disciplined, the human spirit can also be disciplined. When you have followed the recommendations to discipline other aspects of yourself, the discipline of the spirit will become more profitable.

### Consistent Word Intake, Meditation and Practice

To discipline the human spirit, it must be fed with the word of God regularly. After the death of Moses, God taught Joshua how to discipline his spirit in order to be successful. He prescribed a regular dose of the word of God, both in consumption, speaking, and acting on it.

> *This Book of the Law shall not depart from your*
> *mouth, but you shall meditate in it day and night, that*
> *you may observe to do according to all that is written in*
> *it. For then you will make your way prosperous, and*
> *then you will have good success. (Joshua 1:8)*

The Bible also tells us that John the Baptist was also strong in spirit. In other words, he had a disciplined spirit. How did he attain this? Mainly by his consumption of the word of God. Remember that in the days of John, they only had the Old Testament scrolls to refer to. They did not have the New Testament. John the Baptist built up his spirit by mainly hearing, believing, and acting on the word of God that he received.

> *So the child grew and became strong in spirit, and was*
> *in the deserts till the day of his manifestation to Israel.*
> *(Luke 1:80)*

We understand from scriptures that God was speaking to John the Baptist while he was in the desert. In Luke 3:2-6, we read that,

> *while Annas and Caiaphas were high priests, the word*
> *of God came to John the son of Zacharias in the wilder-*
> *ness. And he went into all the region around the Jordan,*
> *preaching a baptism of repentance for the remission of*
> *sins, as it is written in the book of the words of Isaiah*
> *the prophet, saying: "The voice of one crying in the wil-*
> *derness: 'Prepare the way of the LORD; Make His*

*paths straight. Every valley shall be filled and every mountain and hill brought low; the crooked places shall be made straight and the rough ways smooth; and all flesh shall see the salvation of God."'*

In this passage, we see that John received the word that came from God; he believed it and he acted on it. The word that came to him in the wilderness is what he acted on by starting the ministry God called him into.

When you regularly read and meditate on the word of God, and are careful to do what it says you should do, you are building a disciplined spirit. You are developing your spirit, so it can teach your soul to clearly discern good and evil. The Bible defines this as spiritual maturity.

*But solid food belongs to those who are of full age, that is, those who by reason of use have their senses exercised to discern both good and evil. (Hebrews 5:14)*

There are many instructions in the Word of God for the New Testament believer to follow. There are instructions concerning relationships, holiness, love, giving, soul winning, etc., that are in the Bible for us to locate and obey.

Meditating on the word is not the same as memorizing scriptures in order to win a Bible quiz. Meditating on the word helps to take it from your head to your heart. Meditation on the word is what reprograms your thinking to how God wants it to be.

Prayer turns situations around, while meditating on the word turns you around to match what you prayed about.

If you pray more than you meditate on the scriptures, situations will be turned around, but you will remain the same. In a matter of time, the situation will reverse back again to what it used to be.

I encourage you to begin the journey to discipline your spirit today!

## Consistent Worship

Jesus told us that God is seeking those that will worship Him in spirit and in truth. God seeks those kinds of people. If God is seeking those kinds of people, then it means that those kinds of people will be more intensely and frequently exposed to the Holy Spirit.

> *But the hour is coming, and now is, when the true worshipers will worship the Father in spirit and truth; for the Father is seeking such to worship Him. God is Spirit, and those who worship Him must worship in spirit and truth. (John 4:23-24)*

Your spirit longs to worship God. Allow it to do that. Your spirit will positively respond to anointed worship ministrations. As you discipline your spirit to worship God regularly, in spirit and truth, you will soon see yourself waking up with songs of praise to God.

Praise and worship does not only mean singing. Worship is when you render endearments to God. It is when you adore God, exalt Him, thank Him, and honor Him for who He is, what He has done, what He will do, who He is not, and so on.

If you are struggling to praise and worship God, don't panic. Just simply connect to God through the ministry of anointed praise and worship ministers. Through the grace upon their lives that you will contact, you will soon find it easier for you to praise and worship God.

Consciously noting testimonies of God's goodness to you or others that you know, can help trigger thanksgiving to God in your heart.

## Fellowship with the Holy Spirit

Jesus uttered those immortal words when He proclaimed, *"I and My Father are one"* (John 10:30). These words show perfect union and fellowship with the Father through the Holy Spirit.

Training your spirit to be in constant fellowship with the Holy Spirit is very possible, and it carries maximum benefits.

The Holy Spirit is gentle and will not wrestle for our attention; He stands at the door and knocks.

> *Behold, I stand at the door and knock. If anyone hears My voice and opens the door, I will come in to him and dine with him, and he with Me. (Revelation 3:20)*

What is fellowship? Fellowship in our context means companionship.

The Holy Spirit wants to fellowship with us. A disciplined spirit does not only pray when they have needs; it communicates with God throughout the day, through real time thanksgiving, praise and worship, asking questions, and so on.

This communication with the Holy Spirit can be in your understanding, or in your spiritual language, i.e. praying in the spirit. Paul said, *"What is the conclusion then? I will pray with the spirit, and I will also pray with the understanding. I will sing with the spirit, and I will also sing with the understanding. I thank my God I speak with tongues more than you all"* (1 Corinthians 14:15, 18).

Have you ever thought about how God expects us to obey the scriptural injunction in 1 Thessalonians 5:17, to pray without ceasing? One of the way is by praying in the spirit. It is almost impossible to pray in your understanding and fulfill this scripture, keeping in mind that we are to avoid vain repetition.

When you pray in the spirit, you are speaking mysteries. You are arranging things about your life. You are communing with God in its purest form. You are communicating with God in a language that has no limitations. You are praying through. You are edifying your spirit.

Many people complain of their inability to hear from God. Some go as far as saying that they are unable to distinguish the voice of God from the many voices they hear. If that is you reading this book, and you are born again, the starting point for you is to discipline your spirit. As you do this, the voice of God will become more apparent to you.

## Spiritual Authority

In conclusion, a disciplined spirit is one that is under spiritual authority. For more on this, read the book I authored, "The Blessings of being Under Spiritual Authority". It will give you more insight on what it means to be under spiritual authority.

The Godhead has all the power and authority. God, however, delegates that authority to human agents in the family, church, government, workplace, etc. As you legitimately submit to God's authority in those people, you will be disciplining your human spirit. Then and only then can this Bible verse apply to you.

> *For as many as are led by the Spirit of God, these are sons of God. (Romans 8:14)*

A disciplined spirit is the motor that drives the believer. It receives information from the Holy Spirit and/or the Word of God, passes that information to the soul, which then drives the body to obey it.

May the grace of God be abundant upon us all to attain this state of discipline.

# EPILOGUE

Discipline is a virtue that is difficult to imbibe, but comes with immense benefits; It can sometimes be misconstrued as pride. A disciplined person can sometimes be mistaken for a heartless and callous person. A disciplined person can be greatly admired, and also despised at the same time.

A disciplined person puts to death the deeds of the body, but the power to do so is given to us by the Holy Spirit (Romans 8:13).

If man is made up of spirit, soul and body, it goes on to say that if we are to be disciplined, it must be reflected in all these areas of our being, i.e. spirit, soul and body. This is the approach I have taken in this book.

I sincerely believe that if you can understand and apply all the wisdom from this book, to your life, you will no doubt, be a shining star.

I did not emphasize disciplining the mouth in this book, because Jesus said that *"out of the abundance of the heart, his mouth speaks"* (Luke 6:45). A disciplined mouth should be an amplifier of the soul and spirit of a person.

I have a word of caution for you though; attaining the heights espoused in this book must not make you become prideful or condescending to others. You would never have attained it without the help of the Holy Spirit. Watch out for the cancer of pride as you implement the content of this book.

Reject the demonic suggestions that you are better than others because you have been able to master the contents of this book, while others have not been able to.

I declare prophetically that, as you have read this book and will apply the contents therein as enabled by the Holy Spirit, *"you will rise and shine; your light will come; and the glory of God will rise upon you."*

I love you! God loves you more! Bring glory to your Father in Heaven as you keep shining.

# A SINNER'S PRAYER TO RECEIVE JESUS CHRIST AS SAVIOR

Dear Heavenly Father,
I come to You in the Name of Jesus Christ.

You said in Your Word, *"Whosoever shall call upon the name of the Lord shall be saved"* (Romans 10:13). I am calling on Your Name, so I know You have saved me now.

You also said that *"if you confess with your mouth the Lord Jesus and believe in your heart that God has raised Him from the dead, you will be saved. For with the heart one believes unto righteousness, and with the mouth confession is made unto salvation"* (Romans 10:9-10). I believe in my heart Jesus Christ is the Son of God. I believe that He was raised from the dead for my justification, and I confess Him now as my Lord.

Thank You Lord because now I am saved!

Thank You, Lord because I know you have heard my prayer. Thank You, Lord because I am now born again.

Signed _____

Date _____

# ABOUT THE AUTHOR

Emmanuel Adewusi is the Founding and Lead Pastor of Cornerstone Christian Church of God.

Called into ministry with the mandate to "bring restoration and transformation to all by teaching, preaching and demonstrating the gospel of Jesus Christ", he is passionate to see lives restored and transformed to the way God intended from the beginning of creation. He has a passion for the full counsel of the word of God, fellowship with the Holy Spirit and being under spiritual authority.

He hosts several COME AND SEE Conferences, with the goal to reach lost souls for Jesus Christ.

He is also the author of "Now That You Are Born Again, What Next?", "The Blessings of Being Under Spiritual Authority", "The Enlightened Believer", and other inspirational titles.

Emmanuel Adewusi is joyfully married to his wife, Ibukun Adewusi, and together, they are building a thriving Christ-centered family.

# CONTACT THE AUTHOR

I would be delighted to hear from you!

For further inquiries, please contact the author via email: emmanuel.adewusi@cccghq.org.

For online sermons, please visit www.cccghq.org.

# NOTES

# NOTES

# NOTES

26342163R00070